TAKE BACK YOUR LIFE!

Strategic Moves for Overcoming Life's Battles

MARTIN D. ODOM

DEDICATION

This book is dedicated to my wife Nicole who pushed, pulled, prayed for and believed me into completing this project when I almost gave up. She helped me to take back my life and I am forever grateful. She has blessed me with two amazing daughters, Maya Marie Odom, and Samantha Nicole Odom. Thank you girls for being my constant reminder of what really matters in life and for making me laugh… all the time.

Thank You's

I want to thank the people, whose input has been invaluable in helping me think through this work at various stages since it first began as a sermon series in 2006, including: my in-laws Ray and Adrienne Goode, Sis. Barbara Shelton, Bro. Mike McMullen, Rev. DeLishia Boykin, and Pastor Joseph Carlos Robinson.

Finally I want to thank my church family, the Bethel Village AME Church of Harrisburg, PA, an absolutely awesome congregation, for your prayers, patience, confidence, and support. I love you and there is not a thing you can do about it!

CONTENTS

ACKNOWLEDGMENTS

To my father in the ministry Bishop Reginald T. Jackson... For a lifetime of mentorship and friendship.

To my Bishop, the Rt. Rev. Gregory G.M. Ingram...For your encouragement to write, and guidance in completing this work.

To my mentor the late Rev. Dr. Samuel Dewitt Proctor...
For doing far more for me than I ever deserved.

To Bishop Cornal Garnett Henning Sr...For giving me my first big break.

To the late John Nelson Thomas III... For adopting me in the City of New Orleans.

To the late Alvina Roberta Martin Forthner Esq... For being an amazing friend.

To Mom and Dad the late Rev. Dr. L. Sylvester Odom Sr. and Mrs. Loga Isis Butler Odom...For your love, legacy, and model of Christian service.

Chapter One

The Spirit of Fear!

For God has not given us a spirit of fear but of power and of love and of a sound mind.   2 Timothy 1:7 (NKJV)

I Want My Life Back

Is your life out of control? Are you dissatisfied with decisions you have made, dreams deferred, and opportunities you did not take?   If so, you are like many others who have surrendered authority to Satan. Sometimes we turn over our authority all at once. Most of us surrender one painful moment at a time.

Jesus told His disciples in Luke 10:19, "I have given you power to tread on serpents and scorpions, and over all the power of the enemy, and that nothing shall by any means hurt you." Jesus was not just talking to those seventy disciples who had returned to Him joyful over their success in casting out devils in His name. He was talking to us. He was talking to you. Jesus has given you authority over all the power of the enemy. If you have given up that authority it is time to take it back.

Are you ready to take back your life?   This book is for you. You will identify the weapons Satan uses to steal your destiny. These weapons are spirits that attack our spirit and distract us from hungering for God's Holy Spirit. These weapons are spirits that steal life. This book will equip you with strategies to take back your life!

It is Time to Dig Deep

While attending a meeting in Memphis, Tennessee one year, I overheard one of the pastors trying to tell one of the Bishops something he was trying to accomplish was not going to work. He gave the Bishop several good reasons why it would not work. The Bishop described the pastor's problem as a spiritual problem. I did not understand how he could describe the situation as a spiritual problem. I had noticed down through the years the Bishop would often describe problems people brought to him as spiritual. They did not seem particularly spiritual to me. They were problems with finances, transportation, or problems within churches. Mostly they were problems with personalities and egos. Not what you would call spiritual problems.

It took me a while to understand that the Bishop was actually correct. When we peel away the layers of many of the situations that challenge us, we are really dealing with spiritual issues. Ephesians 6:12 says, "Our struggle is not against flesh and blood, but against the rulers, against the powers, against the world forces of this darkness, against the spiritual forces of wickedness in heavenly places." (NASB)

Sometimes it helps to look at your life through a different set of lenses. Spiritual lenses make you understand you can take spiritual authority over the attacks of the enemy. Spiritual lenses help you take back your life.

Too often we don't look at things spiritually because we are looking at them with our natural eyes. The Bible says, "The natural man does not accept the things of the Spirit of God, for they are foolishness to him, and he cannot understand them, because they are spiritually appraised." (1 Corinthians 2:14 NASB) We are like people who decide to build our house on a piece of land. We go through the land and cut down all of the trees but we leave the tree stumps. If all we see are the tree stumps, we think we have taken care of the trees. We are fooled into thinking that the trees are no longer a threat because we can only see stumps. The problem is we really haven't done anything because the tree trunks and the branches were the least of our troubles. The real threat is the roots underneath the stumps that are still alive and spreading under the ground and are able to grow into more trees. Take back your life by dealing with the root of issues that limit, frustrate, and cause you to make decisions you regret.

It is time for us in the body of Christ to deal with some roots. It is time to dig deep. John the Baptist warned the Pharisees and Sadducees the ax had already been laid at the root of the tree. (Matthew 3:10) We also have to take the ax to the root of the tree. The root of many of the issues we struggle with every day is spiritual.

"The devil is busy," is a phrase we often use to describe much of the mess that goes on in our lives. Our cable was cut off, the devil is busy. Our car was repossessed, the devil is busy. We got fired for being late to work one too many times, the devil is busy. Sometimes when hell is breaking loose in our lives and people ask us how we are doing, we reply, *"the devil is busy."* But do you really understand just how busy? If you are going to take back your life, you will have to

understand just how busy the devil really is. The devil is so busy that some of the aliases he is called in the Bible include: the prince of demons, the accuser of the brethren, murderer, and the father of lies. (Revelation 12:10, John 8:44)

You Are Uniquely Qualified

2nd Timothy was written by the Apostle Paul to Timothy a young man he was mentoring in ministry. In this letter Paul is preparing Timothy for how busy the devil can be, even among people who believe in Jesus. One of the biggest lies we believe is the devil spends most of his time around people who don't believe in God. If that were true, he would have never had a reason to bother Job. In fact, if that were the case, the devil would have never tried to tempt Jesus in the wilderness. Nor would so many sincere Christians suffer and struggle with life's battles the way we do. The truth is the devil is busy, and often appears to be busiest among those who follow Christ. Paul shares encouragement and wisdom Timothy will need in his assignment as the pastor of the church at Ephesus.

Paul reminds Timothy of his spiritual heritage. Timothy's grandmother and mother were great workers in the church. He tells Timothy not to try and make it on borrowed religion, but to stir up what God has placed uniquely inside of him. In other words, Paul says maybe your Grandma Lois cooked the best fried chicken the folks in this church ever had. Perhaps your Mother Eunice was one of those church mothers who sang in the choir, worked in the kitchen, served on the board, and comforted the sick. But Timothy, God has given you some gifts that make you unique, and valuable to the work of the Kingdom.

Like Timothy, we all need to be reminded that our Father gives us gifts that uniquely qualify us for a kingdom assignment. As the old folks used to say, "When God made you He broke the mold!"

Sometimes we fall into the trap of comparing ourselves to others and it only makes us vulnerable to Satan's deceit. God has given you something special and necessary in accomplishing His will. What is equally important is what Paul tells Timothy God has not given him. Paul tells Timothy with all of the wonderful gifts God has given you; the one thing God has not given you is a *spirit of fear*. "For God has not given us a spirit of fear but of power and of love and of a sound mind." (2 Timothy 3:7) The *spirit of fear* does not come from God, but we know it is real. Where does it come from? It comes from the devil.

What Do You Fear?

What did Timothy have to fear? He could have feared meeting the same fate as Paul. Paul was writing to him from a Roman prison cell and his crime was spreading the good news of Jesus Christ. The Roman Emperor, Nero, was on a campaign to persecute everyone who followed Jesus. People were being murdered everywhere. Perhaps Timothy had to fear for his life.

Timothy may have feared not living up to the expectations of his mother and grandmother. We do not always feel equipped to live up to the expectations others have set for us. Coming from a family that was so active in church, maybe there was pressure on Timothy to be the next great church worker and he did not want to disappoint.

Timothy could fear all of the false teachers and people with strange ideas that would challenge him as he gave leadership to that congregation. Maybe Timothy would have been fearful of what people might say or think about him as he sought to stir up and use the gifts God had given him. Everybody is not always happy when you use the gifts God has given you. Some people get angry, and some people get ugly when you use what God has given you. Some people, whom we will discuss later, become plain old jealous because you are being the person God called you to be.

It shouldn't be hard for us to imagine Timothy feared some things. What does anybody fear? What do you fear? Do you fear that if you take a risk and reach for your dream you will fail and be labeled a failure for the rest of your life? Do you fear starting over and being ridiculed by people who you thought were your friends when they see you trying to do something different with your life? Do you fear confronting a person or situation in your life you have ignored for years hoping it would go away or get better? What do you fear? Take back your life by admitting what you fear so you can confront and conquer it. None of us can conquer what we will not confront.

The *spirit of fear* is as powerful today as it was in the days of Paul and Timothy. I am not talking about the fear of heights, water, spiders or other normal human anxieties. Even those fears can become unusually intense and steal life from us. Paul understood that Timothy had important work to do for God. He also knew the enemy has more than one way to prevent us from getting to where God wants to take us.

Better Late than Never

Have you ever been going somewhere and come to a point where you could not go the way you knew to go, so you had to make a turn? When you made the turn and thought you could get back on track, you realized the street you turned onto did not get you where you wanted to go! Finally, after about 25 minutes, you realize you are totally out of the way. That really happened to me while traveling. I was in Philadelphia, PA, and I left the hotel going to a meeting. I got to the meeting 45 minutes late. My host just smiled when I apologized for being late and informed him I had taken an involuntary tour of the city that morning. When you are going somewhere in God, your enemy the devil, has a lot of turns, one way streets, detours, and dead ends to prevent you from getting to where God is taking you.

Excuse me while I testify, I was late but I got there. I had some detours along the way, but I got there. The devil took me down some dead end relationships and some dead end decisions, but I made it over. I got turned around and frustrated so I almost decided to go back to where I came from, but I got there. Haven't you ever tried to go somewhere and been so frustrated in going you said forget about this, "I am going back to where I came from?"

I don't know about you, but if I would have gone back to where I came from, I probably would not be here today. If I had gone back to where I came from, I might be dead today. I might be in prison today. I might be strung out on drugs right now. If I had gone back to where I came from, who knows where I would be. I am only here today because of the goodness of

God that kept me in spite of my shortcomings.

My first job was working for a lady in our neighborhood who owned a fruit truck with her husband. I was 14 years old. It paid $60.00 a week and all of the fruit I could carry home at the end of the day. Some of the other boys who worked on the truck used to tease me, because I was not as advanced in the ways of the streets as they were. I shall never forget during one of those teasing sessions the lady interrupted them and told them to leave me alone, because I could not help it if I was a *"late bloomer"*. She meant well, but being called a *"late bloomer"* didn't help my case with the other boys.

When I look back on my life and see the path God put me on and consider the path I could have taken, I say glory to God for being a *"late bloomer"*. Take back your life by understanding in spite of the detours the enemy put in your path you still have a testimony if you are able to say *better late than never*.

Paul understood that Timothy had important work to do for God. He knew we have an enemy who has more than one way of trying to prevent us from going where God is taking us. Paul had seen some of his other helpers destroyed by the enemy. The Bible tells us about a man named Demas. He was one of Paul's companions, but Brother Demas got hold of a long - legged woman that messed him up. Maybe it was not a woman. Perhaps it was a good bottle of scotch, or one of those Mediterranean casinos that caused Demas to miss his opportunity. Paul is not specific except to say that Brother Demas got messed up because he got out there in the world and he liked what he saw. (2 Timothy 4:10) Paul also knew the helpers he had in Asia, two men named Phygellus and Hermogenes had for whatever reason been turned away. (2 Timothy 1:15) Paul understood the enemy had many different methods of trying to detour Timothy from his destiny.

Paul tells Timothy with all that is facing and confronting you, I know the temptation to allow fear to hinder you will be great. God has given you many gifts. Whenever the *spirit of fear* shows up in your life, you need to understand it is not from God and it is not for your good.

The Anatomy of Fear

Like Timothy, you and I also have important work to do for God. Whether that work is preaching from a pulpit, or raising your children to know the Lord. Whether singing the solo for the choir, or going to work every day and providing for your family. Whether it is being an officer or leader in your church, or being that person of integrity on your job people know they can come to when they need a word of prayer or advice. Our Father has given you special gifts because He has important work for you to do. The *spirit of fear* is not a gift from God. It is a trap from your enemy, the devil. What do you fear?

Some of us fear being exposed. What if people find out how we really are? What if people knew that we are not what we appear to be? Well, first of all, what people? The same people who are not really what they appear to be? Some of us fear failure and rejection. What if we try something and it doesn't work? What if I step out on faith and put myself out there; expose myself to this person or these people? What if they say I am not good enough? Some of us fear success. What if I am good at this? What if I like it? What if I enjoy it and have to re-evaluate what I thought I already knew about myself?

Fear is a spirit. It is not an emotion. It is not a natural part of who we are. The *spirit of fear* is one of the weapons our enemy, Satan, uses to keep you and I stuck in a place where we are not useful to God, ourselves, or one another.

Fear represents the absence, or lack of faith in God. When Jesus was out on the lake with His disciples and the storm came in Mark Chapter 4, the disciples woke Jesus up and essentially said 'Man we are about to die here! Can You please do something?' Jesus said, "Why are you fearful, O you of little faith?" (Mark 4:40) Fear is so detrimental because it can cause you to question whether God cares about you. The disciples had Jesus in the boat with them but they asked this question, "Master carest thou not that we are perishing?" (Mark 4:38) Fear steals life from you when it causes you to question whether God cares about you. Take back your life by refusing to let fear of your circumstances make you question God's love for you.

When the spirit of fear is in control of your life you make unproductive choices. People get crazy when they fear someone will take their job. When a person fears that someone might take their spouse they become irrational. When the spirit of fear has control of us our decisions are not rational, and they don't give God glory. Take back your life by taking authority over the *spirit of fear*.

I do not agree with what some psychologists and psychotherapists teach us about fear. They teach that fear is simply an emotion, like anger, happiness, or hope. They teach that fear is already within us and is located within an area of our brain called the amygdala. When the amygdala receives certain stimuli this triggers a series of reactions and signals from our brain that cause us to become fearful.

With deference to those who give themselves to the study of the human mind, the Bible says fear is a spirit and it does not come from God! It is not in our DNA! It is not in our genetic make - up! Fear is not part of our mental faculties! Fear is a spirit and it does not come from God! Since it is a spirit that means it is real, it is active, it is alive, but it does not have a body. If you and I decide we will not serve as its hosts then the *spirit of fear* will have to go someplace else.

Jesus encountered a man with unclean spirits who said his name was Legion because of the many unclean spirits that were in him. (Mark 5:9) When Jesus cast them out of the man the demons begged Jesus to send them into the swine so they would have something to serve as their host. (Mark 5:12) God has not given us the *spirit of fear*. Take back your life by making the *spirit of fear* an unwelcome visitor.

You are already equipped with what you need to overcome *the spirit of fear*. Paul tells Timothy I remember the faith your grandmother and mother had, "and I am persuaded is in you also." Paul is saying Timothy you are a person of faith and a person of faith does not have anything to fear. When we start believing Jesus has bought our salvation with His own blood then the *spirit of fear* has no place in our life. Fear is for people who don't know God. If you know God, and God knows you, then even if it's more than you can handle, it's not more than God can handle. I love the way the writer of Psalm 27 reminds us why we have no reason to fear. "The Lord is my light and my salvation; Whom shall I fear? The Lord is the defense of my life; Whom shall I dread?" (Psalm 27:1 NASB) Stop telling God how big your problems are and start telling your problems how big our God is.

Fear is Not a Factor

This type of faith is what prompted David to resound, "Yea, though I walk through the valley of the shadow of death I will fear no evil." (Psalm 23: 4) Why David? Is it because evil isn't real? No! Is it because evil isn't menacing? No! Is it because evil isn't dangerous? No! It is because God is with me. If God is with me, God won't wait until my enemy turns his back to bless me. God won't wait until my enemy gets tired, and says I do not feel like fighting anymore, to bless me. God won't wait until my enemy has gotten all he wants and doesn't want any more in order to bless me. If God is with me, David says, "He will prepare a table before me in the presence of my enemies." (Psalm 23:5)

Don't be afraid to let God bless you! God will bless you when people don't even like you! God will bless you when people are busy talking about your past and what you did 15 years ago! God will bless you when other people think they should have been the one getting your blessing! Don't let fear stop you from going where God is taking you. There used to be a television program that helped people to face their fears. They had the contestants eat all kinds of crazy stuff like worms, and do all kinds of activities. The winner would be congratulated on overcoming their fears. I'm so glad you and I don't have to eat what the devil wants to feed us. We don't have to accept the devil's challenges to prove anything. If you had a life changing encounter with Jesus one day let me be the first to tell you congratulations, you have already won.

Expect to Take Some Hits!

The power the *spirit of fear* has over us is we are afraid of the consequences of the things we fear. But the Good News of turning your life over to Jesus is those consequences are of no real consequence to believers. The prophet Jeremiah said once we open the door to the *spirit of fear,* the actual fear does more harm than the thing we fear. "The one who flees from the terror will fall into the pit, and the one who climbs out of the pit will be caught in the snare." (Jeremiah 48:44 NASB) In other words the only reason the *spirit of fear* can exercise any influence, or power in your life is it prevents you from doing things that will cause you to take some hits in life. But you are going to take some hits no matter what you do in life. Take back your life by recognizing you are going to take some hits, and it is okay.

Paul says, "God has not given us a spirit fear but of power of love and of a sound mind." (2 Timothy 1:7) Paul is writing from a prison cell. Someone tells him when to eat and when to sleep. Someone tells him what to wear and at what times he can go and stretch his legs. He is not in control of any of the aspects of his own life that are normally associated with being in control. Paul is writing from prison and seems to be powerless. Yet he writes to Timothy and tells him that in Christ we are powerful.

Paul does not sugar coat his message to

Timothy. He tells him in this life everybody is not going to like you all the time. Everybody will not agree with you all of the time. Everybody will not think you are right all of the time, nor will everybody think you are wonderful all of the time. If you spend all of your time worried about who does not think you are wonderful, you will be paralyzed by the *spirit of fear*. Paul is honest about his own life. He says yes, I am in prison. Yes, I have had some mistreatment. Yes, some of the people I thought I could depend on have let me down. Paul is honest about it. He says yes, Timothy I took some hits along the way and so will you. But guess what? Getting hit is not the end of the world.

I'm Hit But I'm Holding!

Take authority over the *spirit of fear* in your life by accepting the fact you are going to take some hits along the way. It was not that you lost your job; it was that you took a hit. It was not that your marriage fell apart; it was that you took a hit. It was not that your child went down the wrong road; it was that you took a hit. It does not matter who you are, all of us are going to take some hits along the way. Jesus promised, "In this world you will have trouble, but be of good courage for I have overcome the world." (John 16:33)

Growing up in Newark, NJ we would play football outside in the street. Sometimes the quarterback would throw the ball to a receiver. While they were going to catch the ball, they would hear the footsteps of the person coming to hit them as soon as they caught the ball. In that split second when they should have had their mind on catching the ball, they would put their mind on preparing for the impact of the hit. Do you know what happens? You end up getting hit while missing or dropping the ball. You still got hit, but you dropped the ball. I want to be able to say in my life that I took the hit, but held on to the ball. I took the hit, but didn't give up on my dream. I took the hit, but held on to my vision. I took the hit, but my spouse and I are still together. I took the hit, but now my child is in church praising the Lord. Cancer thought it had me but I didn't lose my mind. I took the hit, but held on to the ball.

In the Name and the Blood of Jesus, I bind the *spirit of fear* in your life today. It has no power over you. It has no place in your life because you are not afraid to take the hit. That's what Paul was really saying to Timothy. Yes, you will get hit, but hold on. I'm in prison but I'm holding on. I have been beaten but I am holding on. I have been disappointed but I'm holding on. I have been misunderstood but I am holding on. I have been misrepresented but I'm holding on. I took a hit and I even heard the footsteps coming but I held on to the ball.

Take authority over the *spirit of fear* in your life. Take back your life by saying I hear the footsteps but I'm going to keep on praising Jesus. I hear the footsteps but I'm going to keep on serving the Lord. I hear the footsteps but I'm holding on to my faith, holding on to my praise, and holding on to what my Father has given me. Taking the hit but holding on to what God has deposited in you is taking back your life.

Prayer: Father I bind the *spirit of fear* in my life, in the Name of Jesus. I know fear is not part of me, and it does not come from You. When I feel afraid I will ask you to strengthen my faith. Help me to hold on to Your promises, and to trust You despite the hits I may take. I am more than a conqueror through Christ who loves me, and no weapon that is formed against me will prosper in Jesus Name. Amen!

Chapter Two

The Spirit of Doubt!

And immediately Jesus stretched out His hand and took hold of him and said to him, "O you of little faith, why did you doubt?" Matthew 14:31 (NASB)

Know Your Enemy

Taking back your life means recognizing who is trying to steal life from you and how he operates. Our enemy has many names; the devil, Satan, Beelzebub, and Lucifer. Stop wasting time worrying about who you dislike, hate, or think is your enemy. Your real enemy is the devil.

That person on your job is not your enemy. You may not like their work ethic, but that does not make them your enemy. You may think she wears her skirts too short. You may not like the way he kisses up to the boss, but that person is not your enemy. Nor is the person who lives down the street from you, or goes to your church. You may know something about them that makes you dislike them. Even better, they may know something about you that makes you dislike them.

Much of the "disliking" that goes on is not nearly as much about what we know about someone else and how fake they are, as it is about what others know about us. We know about them because we were in the same place they were, and neither of us had any business being there. It was not just that we saw them, they also saw us. That person is not your enemy. Your enemy is not the person who says something mean to you or nasty about you. Your enemy is not the person

18

who you were competing with for the same man, woman, job, or recognition. Your enemy is not your ex-wife or ex-husband. Your enemy is the devil. The devil is your enemy and he is out to steal life from you.

Another Cowardly Lion!

Our enemy is a fallen angel, (Luke 10: 18) who is out to kill, steal, and destroy. (John 10:10) Our enemy has a purpose which is to prevent, hinder, distract, and discourage us from achieving our purpose in God. Peter describes him as being "like a roaring lion seeking someone to devour." (I Peter 5:8)

If you watch nature programs on television about lions, you have noticed at least three characteristics of how lions attack a herd of gazelles or other prey. First, they attack in groups. Your enemy loves to attack by sending more than one problem or situation into your life at once. I can just about promise you that hell at home will almost always be accompanied by hell at work. Hell at work will almost always attack when your body is under physical attack from sickness. Sickness will almost always show up while you are also trying to handle a financial crisis. Lions attack in groups. In one single day Job lost his oxen, donkeys, servants, sheep, camels, and all of his children due to the attack of the enemy. (Job 1:13-19)

Secondly, lions attack the smallest, weakest, and slowest in the group. Your enemy will always look to attack you in your moments of spiritual vulnerability. After Satan tried unsuccessfully to tempt Jesus in the wilderness the Bible says, "He departed from Him until an opportune time." (Luke 4:13) That means the devil wasn't leaving Jesus alone, he was just waiting to catch

Jesus at a vulnerable moment. Has the devil ever caught you at a vulnerable moment? It was not an accident; he was waiting until an opportune time. Lions specialize in catching the one who can't keep up with the rest of the herd, or the one they can separate from the herd.

Lastly, your enemy will always seek to attack you when you are alone, lonely, or going through a period when you are isolating yourself from the body of Christ. I tell people all of the time, don't let the devil catch you in a back alley by yourself. In the back alley alone in the dark, he can beat on you like there is no tomorrow. Make him catch you on Main Street where you have some help. That simply means when we go through seasons of attack, depression, and despair we should not hide from church, and from those who love and care about us. That is what the devil wants us to do.

A Virus on the Loose!

How does Satan accomplish his purpose? He accomplishes his purpose by affecting, infecting, and inflicting us with demonic spirits. Think of yourself as a human computer. Computers are wonderful instruments. Computers are used to accomplish great things. Computers are crucial to some of the great advances in medicine and science. However, no matter how good a computer you have, if you let that computer get a virus, one virus can wipe that computer out. One virus can erase a lifetime of work. One virus can cause that computer to lose its memory and take what was built for good and wipe it all away. One virus can allow someone to steal your identity and important information about you that can make your life a living hell.

Haven't you ever been wiped out by a virus? Tell the truth! Haven't you ever opened up a file in your life you wish you had never opened? One virus can cause us to forget everything we know. One virus can cause us to forget how good God has been to us and how God has made a way out of no way in our lives. One virus can make us lose our minds. One virus can steal life from you.

We are like computers, capable of being used for great things, but susceptible to being messed up by little things. What are those things which possibly prevent us from reaching our potential? They are spirits which the enemy sows into our lives to cause us to crash. One of the most harmful viruses Satan uses on us is the *spirit of doubt.* He even used it on a disciple of Jesus.

Peter the Rock

The Gospels share more about Jesus' relationship with Peter than His relationship with any of the other disciples. We know about the ambition of James and John. They asked Jesus if they could sit one on His right hand and the other on His left hand when He came into His kingdom. (Mark 10:37) We know a little more about Judas because of the flaws in his character that give us clues all along to his betrayal of Jesus. We saw how jealous Judas became when the woman anointed Jesus' feet with perfume. (John 12:4-5) We know that Andrew was a great evangelist because he went and recruited his brother Simon. Jesus gave Simon the name Peter, which means the rock. We know that Matthew, also known as Levi, had been a tax collector, which was an unpopular profession.

Peter is different because Jesus speaks directly

to him throughout the gospels. Jesus said, "You are Peter, and upon this rock I will build My church; and the gates of Hades shall not overpower it." (Matthew 16:18 NASB) When all of the other disciples were saying who they thought Jesus was Peter said, "Thou art the Christ, the Son of the Living God." (Matthew 16:16 NASB) Jesus' reply to Peter tells us much about the anointing that was on Peter's life. "Flesh and blood did not reveal this to you but My Father who is in heaven." (Matthew 16:17 NASB)

In Peter, Jesus recognized the devil's foothold when he said, "Get behind Me, Satan, you are a stumbling block to Me." (Matthew 16:23 NASB) Even the enemy recognized Peter's potential. Jesus told Peter, "Satan has demanded permission to sift you like wheat; but I have prayed for you that your faith may not fail; and you, when once you have turned again, strengthen your brothers." (Luke 22:31-32 NASB)

Peter's Bout With Doubt!

In Matthew Chapter 14, Jesus says something to Peter that really helps us to understand and recognize how powerful and dangerous the *spirit of doubt* can be in our lives. Jesus sent everyone, including His disciples away so He could have some quiet time with God. Jesus reminds us we all need quiet time with God. No matter how well you believe you have it all together, if you are not spending any quiet time with God, you are a crash waiting to happen. He goes up into a mountain to pray and His disciples get into a boat to go over to the other side of the water.

While they were out there in the sea, a storm arose and the boat was tossed by the winds and there was a heavy or contrary wind. This went on for several hours. After a while, they saw Jesus walking on the sea as though He were walking on dry ground. The Bible says they were afraid because they thought Jesus was a ghost. Jesus identified Himself to the disciples but Peter said "Lord if it is You; command me to come to You on the water." (Matthew 14:28 NASB)

The Joys and Perils of Water Walking!

Jesus tells Peter to come and Peter begins to walk toward Jesus on the water. When Peter got out of the boat and began walking on the water, he saw heavy wind, became afraid, and began to sink. Peter cried out to Jesus, "Lord, save me." (Matthew 14:30 NASB) The Bible says immediately Jesus caught his hand and said these powerful and poignant words to Peter, "O you of little faith, why did you doubt?" (Matthew 14:31 NASB)

In the New Testament Greek this word doubt is distazo, which means to waiver. It implies having been sure of something then becoming unsure. It means to go back and forth. *'Peter, you were there, why did you doubt?'*

Peter was on the verge of something major? The Bible says, "Peter got out of the boat and walked on the water and came toward Jesus." (Matthew 14:29 NASB) This is Peter we are talking about, not Jesus. Peter was just an ordinary man. He was not fully human and fully God like Jesus. He was just fully human like us. Peter was not endowed with an extraordinary formal education. He was not an educated scholar like Paul. He was just ordinary Peter.

Peter walked on the water to go toward Jesus. Do you know you don't have to be a famous person or a big person for God to do something great in you? You don't have to go to an Ivy League school, for God to do something great in you! You don't have to come from a certain family, have a certain last name, or grow up in a certain section of town, for God to do something great in you. God can do something great in you, even if you come from the wrong side of the tracks. God can do something great in you, whether you are *ghetto fabulous* or *trailer trash*. God can do something great in you, whether you were a teenage mother, or an ex-drug dealer. Do you understand that Peter was on the verge of doing something spectacular?

The disciples had seen Jesus make the blind see and the deaf hear. They had seen Jesus make the lame walk, and feed the multitude without enough food to feed the twelve of them. They had seen Jesus heal sick people, and do all types of miracles. They had even seen Jesus speak to another storm and the wind and the waves obeyed Him. Now they had seen Jesus walk on the water.

But this is not Jesus we are talking about, this is Peter. Peter walked on the water. Peter is walking in the supernatural. He is doing something he is not able to do by himself and is not supposed to be able to do at all. Peter is walking on water! Just when he begins to walk into the supernatural power of God in his own life he sees the wind. (Matthew 14:30 NASB) The *spirit of doubt* creeps in, and he cannot believe what he is doing himself, and he begins to fall into the water. Take back your life by refusing to see the wind. If Peter had never looked at the wind, just imagine what else might have happened that day. We pick and choose what we want to see every day. We look at people and we only see the good in them or the bad in them. They are not all good or all bad; we are just choosing to see what we want.

You can choose not to see the wind. You can choose not to see the negative attitudes around you. You can choose not to see the looks of discouragement and low expectations others may have for you. All of these things are nothing but wind anyway.

Can I tell you about the *spirit of doubt*? Doubt is disbelief of what we know to be true because it does not make sense? The *spirit of doubt* shows up in your life because you are about to start walking into some areas in which God wants to bless you so much that it does not make sense. When the enemy starts sowing the *spirit of doubt* into your spirit, it is because the enemy does not want you to believe that God can do what God is doing in your life. The enemy wants you to believe that this is too good to be true, when really it is too much like God not to be true.

Peter has enough faith to get out of the boat in the middle of the storm and start walking on the water toward Jesus. He has overcome the *spirit of fear*. He is not afraid of the consequences of getting out of the boat. But when he gets out of the boat and starts walking in the spiritual authority Jesus has given him; the *spirit of doubt* causes him to disbelieve what God is doing in his life. That is one of the ways the enemy steals life from us by causing us to doubt what God is doing in our lives. Take back your life by believing that our Father wants to bless you "exceeding, abundantly beyond all that we ask or think." (Ephesians 3:20 NASB)

Peter is really saying, *'there is no way I should be walking on water, especially in this wind.'* Can I tell you when doubt shows up? Doubt shows up when the same doctor that said you only had six months to live is the same doctor that tells you I'm sorry but I can't find anything wrong with you. Something was there, I know it was, I saw it but it is not there anymore. Doubt shows up when the same person you had given up on a long time ago, and decided God must not have heard or answered your prayers, turns their life around and starts over. When that person gives their life to the Lord and begins again, doubt will show up. Doubt shows up when God gives us the house our credit could not attain, the job our education or experience does not merit, or the opportunity our mean and spiteful ways do not deserve.

The *spirit of doubt* will cause us to disbelieve what we know is true because it does not make sense to us. Are you ready to walk on water today? Are you ready to walk into the supernatural power of God, and receive what God wants to give you even if it does not make sense? God wants to give us more than a nice car and a good job. God wants to give us more than a big house and fancy title. God wants to give us more than a rich husband or a pretty wife. God wants to give us supernatural power. God has power for us to overcome, and rebuke the devourer, deceiver, and whisperer in our lives. God wants to give us power to do more than even makes sense to us. Doubt will show up in our lives at times when God is moving, so we don't believe what we know is true just because it does not make sense.

The enemy couldn't stop Peter from getting out

of the boat and walking towards Christ. But by using the *spirit of doubt* while Peter was walking on the water, the enemy could prevent Peter from being a powerful witness to all of those who would have gained new faith and courage by seeing him walk on the water toward Jesus. When Peter started doubting and started falling, what do you think the other disciples in the boat were thinking? *'Well, I better not try that because I might fall like Peter.'* Maybe the enemy can't stop you from coming to church and beginning your walk toward Jesus. But when the supernatural power of God begins to work in your life your enemy will try to sow doubt into your spirit so nobody else will decide to come to Jesus.

When you overcome the *spirit of doubt* you take back your life, while strengthening those who are watching you to take back their lives as well. Always remember while you are exercising your faith somebody else is watching. Those other disciples were looking at Peter and someone is going to be influenced to trust God or to lose faith because they are watching you.

If You Are In a Storm Expect Wind!

Jesus asks Peter a penetrating question, "O you of little faith, why did you doubt?" (Matthew 14:31 NASB) "Why did you doubt?" *'Hey Peter, you knew you were in a storm. You should have expected some wind. You have been out here for hours trying to survive this storm and now I have come out here. Why, did you doubt? I didn't ask you to get out of the boat. You asked Me to command you to come. Why did you doubt?'*

If you can recognize the fact that you are in a storm, whether it is a family storm, financial storm, health storm, emotional storm, or all of the above; you should expect some strong winds to blow. There will be some challenges and obstacles. If you are in the storm and you are crazy enough to step out of where you are, and start walking toward Jesus; why doubt that God is moving in your life simply because there are still obstacles?

We often think because we start taking steps towards Jesus our life is going to instantly be perfect. All of our problems will be over and we won't have any of the obstacles we were facing that caused us to call out to Jesus in the first place. That is the enemy using doubt in our lives. We start walking towards Jesus and Jesus starts working miracles in our life. We see the winds blowing, and start to doubt Jesus is doing what we know He is doing in our lives. Jesus told His disciples, "If anyone would come after Him he had to deny himself, take up his own cross daily and follow Him." (Luke 9:23) Discipleship is a daily choice to follow Jesus. It is a daily choice to pick up your own cross. Taking back your life is not a one-time fix. It is a daily choice to overcome doubt by believing "all things are possible to those who believe." (Mark 9:23 NASB)

Why would you doubt? It is as though Jesus is saying to Peter, *'hey Peter what are you stupid? You got out of the boat in the middle of the water in the midst of a storm. Did you think there was not going to be any wind?'* If you were the biggest drug dealer in town, and now you are in church turning your life around, and the thug life is the only life you ever knew; do you think there won't be any winds blowing? It will be a daily choice and challenge for you. If you were the loosest woman in town, and now you are in church singing in the choir, serving on the usher board, going to Bible study; did you think there would not be any winds blowing? It will be a daily choice and challenge for you. Just because you start tithing does not automatically clear up 25 years of bad credit and unwise spending choices. Of course there will be some winds. Tithing does unleash God's supernatural power in your finances. It does not mean along the way there will not be some obstacles, even some setbacks, and some hits.

If Jesus has started moving in our lives, we should expect some wind to blow. Of course wind is going to blow when we are in the midst of a storm. Don't let your enemy short circuit what God is doing in your life just because wind starts blowing. I told you in the first chapter to expect to take some hits. Now I am telling you to expect to experience some wind. Take back your life by not being surprised by adversity. The Bible does not say few are the afflictions of the righteous, the Bible says, "many are the afflictions of the righteous, but the Lord delivers him from them all." (Psalm 34:19)

Don't Doubt Your Miracle!

Jesus also seems to ask Peter, why out of all His disciples he would be the one to doubt? *'I might have expected one of the others to doubt, but Peter, not you. After all we have been through. After all you have seen me do. Why Peter of all people, did you doubt?'* Taking authority over the *spirit of doubt* in our lives means believing when God is doing something great in us. Claim Your Miracle!

Peter had already seen Jesus heal his mother in law, a leper, and a centurion's servant. He had already seen Jesus cast out demons, and heal multitudes of people. Peter had already seen Jesus make the wind and the waves obey Him, heal a man who could not walk, make two blind men see, and a mute man speak. Now, when it came to Jesus working a miracle in Peter's life, not his mother in law, or friends, or people he knew, Peter had a problem claiming his own miracle. Taking back your life requires being more than a spectator and cheerleader for others in the supernatural promises of our Father. It requires you to believe the miracle God is working in your life.

It is wonderful to see God do great miracles in the lives of others, but at some point you have to believe God is willing and able to do the spectacular in your life.

I Want My Miracle!

I like what Peter says at first, he is there in the boat and he essentially says, *'Jesus I have seen You work these miracles in everybody else's life but right now; out here on this water in the middle of this storm; if it is really You, I want my miracle.'* Are you crazy enough to tell the Lord today I want my miracle? Lord I'm claiming my miracle. Lord here I am in the midst of a storm, and there is no better time for a miracle than this. Don't give me a miracle on the dry ground while everything is going fine. Give me my miracle in the midst of my storm because that is when I need a miracle.

What does Peter do? He gets halfway through his miracle, he is walking on the water, and he allows the *spirit of doubt* to short-change him of his miracle. Peter is like so many of us today. We believe God can work miracles in anybody else's life. When it comes to accepting the miracle God is working in our lives, we allow the *spirit of doubt* to rob us of what we know to be true. We are cynical. We brace ourselves for disappointment rather than positioning ourselves for a miracle. When we see God moving in our lives in supernatural ways, we are automatically programmed to disbelieve what God is doing in our lives.

We are like that father who came to Jesus to heal his son. Jesus told him all things were possible to those who believed. The father replied, "Lord I believe, but help my unbelief." (Mark 9:24) Come on now! Do you need help with your unbelief today? In what area of your life do you need a miracle that is being blocked by your unbelief?

If you are going through a storm right now, then speak to that *spirit of doubt* and say don't try to hold me back. I am about to become a water walker. I want my miracle. If you see me walking on water, don't be angry, or remind me I am not a good swimmer. Don't tell me I am in the middle of a storm. I already know I am in a storm and that's why I'm ready for a miracle. Take authority over the *spirit of doubt* in your life. Admit you are in a storm and claim your miracle.

We can pretend as though we are not in some storms if we choose, but we are only fooling ourselves. We can act like the sun is shining and everything is beautiful if we want, but we are only delaying the miracle God wants to work in our lives. We put on a mask that says; I just have a beautiful perfect marriage, all my kids are on the honor roll and doing fine.

Everybody in my family is doing wonderful and has a clean bill of health. All of my bills are paid, and I don't have a care in the world. It is a lie that we tell ourselves and others. Real people, who are in real storms, and have real situations beyond their control, have no problem crying out, I am in the midst of a storm and I want my miracle!

Remember When

Jesus asks Peter, "why did you doubt?" He was saying, *'Peter, Peter, Peter, of all of the things you could have possibly done, how could you of all things doubt? How could you not believe what you know to be true?'* Take back your life by learning from your storms. This was not the first storm Peter had been in with Jesus. In the eighth chapter of Matthew, Jesus was on the boat with the disciples when a storm came. Jesus was asleep and they woke him up saying, "Save us Lord; we are perishing." (Matthew 8:25 NASB) Jesus asked, "Why are you timid, you men of little faith?" (Matthew 8:26 NASB) Then Jesus spoke to the storm and the winds and the rain ceased.

In Matthew Chapter 14 the disciples are on the boat again, and Jesus is not with them this time, but Jesus shows up. I know that's the truth, because Jesus showed up in the midst of my storm one day. I cannot even begin to tell you just how many times Jesus has shown up in the midst of storms in my life. But if you think about your own life you will have to admit Jesus has shown up in some storms in your life too. Jesus shows up in the midst of the storm and Peter says, "Lord, if it is You, command me to come to You on the water." (Matthew 14:28 NASB) Peter had already seen Jesus in action in one storm. He had already seen that the winds and the waves would obey Jesus. While Peter was midway through his miracle the *spirit of doubt* caused him to worry about something he had already seen Jesus control in the previous storm.

It seems like Peter would have been able to walk into his miracle without worrying about what the winds were doing, because he knew he was walking to the wind keeper. Take back your life by hitting the rewind button and looking back at the storms the Lord has already brought you through. When David volunteered to go and fight the giant Goliath, people thought he was crazy. Everyone else was afraid of Goliath, but David experienced victory that day, because David hit rewind and said. "The Lord who delivered me from the paw of the lion and from the paw of the bear, He will deliver me from the hand of this Philistine." (1 Samuel 17:37 NASB)

Some of us have been through enough storms in our lives by now to know without a doubt Jesus will keep us in the midst of the storm. What about you? Have you been through enough storms by now to know Jesus will bring you safely through? Are you under the impression you survived the most difficult moments of your life because of something you did? Or do you recognize it was the hand of a loving Savior who gently guided you through? Jesus says, *'Peter, Why did you doubt? After all we have been through. After you saw what I did the last time, how could you doubt just because a little wind started blowing?'* Take back your life by taking authority over the spirit of doubt in your life.

The next time you are in a storm start remembering what happened the last time you were in a storm.   The same God who brought you out of that storm is the same God who will bring you out of this storm. Why did you doubt?

If you remembered what happened in the last storm, you were positioned for a miracle in this storm. If you remembered what happened in your last storm, God was about to take you to another level in this storm. If you remembered what happened in the last storm, you were about to start walking in the supernatural in this storm. I know without a doubt He will bring me through this storm because He brought me through the last one. I know Satan may try to trick me. I know the devil may try to cause me to lose my memory. I know the enemy may try to make the wind blow louder to try and make me lose my focus, but I know He watches me.

When my wife and I went on our honeymoon we were blessed to go to the island of Aruba. While there on the island I noticed something about the beach. I loved the sand, and I absolutely loved the sky blue water in which I could see my toes. There was only one aspect of the island that concerned me. There were no life guards on duty along the beach we were on. I am used to going to beaches where there are always life guards on duty. The danger of being at a beach with no lifeguards is no matter how good of a swimmer you are sometimes the current is stronger than you realize. It is very easy to look up and find yourself much farther out than you expected. But I am glad to know that when I find myself in the deep waters of life, we have a life guard who is always on duty. We have a life guard who is always watching. We can never drift so far out that He cannot save us. We have no reason to ever doubt

34

because His eyes are ever upon us.

If we are like computers and one virus can cause us to lose our memory and forget how good God has been, then we need some anti- virus software for the soul. The only anti - virus software for the soul is the Word of God. Read God's Word every day. Eat it for breakfast and digest it all day long. Underline, highlight, and memorize verses of your Bible. Fill your memory with His promises and let our Savior Jesus work in your life today. Take back your life by overcoming doubt with His Word.

Prayer: Heavenly Father, I cancel the devils' assignment in my life. I rebuke the *spirit of doubt* when it rises up against me. I refuse to let doubt cause me to miss my miracle. I want my miracle. In the Name of Jesus I ask You to remind me of the many storms You have already brought me through, whenever doubt tempts me to lose faith in the face of storm. You told me in Your Word that in this world I would have trouble, but I could be of good courage because Jesus has overcome the world. I expect storms, and I expect to overcome in Jesus Name. Amen!

Chapter Three

The Spirit of Self – Destruction!

For the good that I wish I do not do; but I practice the very
evil that I do not wish. Romans 7:19 (NKJV)

Taking back your life by overcoming the spirit
of fear and doubt is a major accomplishment. Your
enemy, the devil, will not be satisfied until he tests you
with one of the most devastating weapons in his
arsenal, the *spirit of self-destruction*. One of my
favorite television programs when I was growing up
was *Mission Impossible*. I liked the music. I liked the
idea of the show, espionage and the way it was all put
together. I liked the fact if you watched more than one
or two episodes you knew no matter how impossible
the mission seemed they were going to find a way to
get it done. I also liked the way they would set up each
episode. The main character would get a tape and play
it in his car. Sometimes you would see him listening to
it, and sometimes you would just hear the voice on the
tape playing. At the conclusion of the tape the voice
would say your mission, if you decide to accept it, is
such and such, and then it would say this tape will self-
destruct in five seconds. There was something in that
tape that was programmed to self-destruct. There was
an explosive inside of the tape. After it played the
message, it would automatically blow up. The man
would throw the tape out of the car window, or get rid
of it in some crazy way, and go out to accomplish the
impossible.

Five Seconds to a Boom!

Sometimes all we have between a decision that
leads to self-destruction and doing what we know is

right is about five seconds. Sometimes about five seconds is all we have between saying *'meet me at the hotel, and saying I am going home to my wife and children.'* Sometimes about five seconds is all we have between saying, *'pass the blunt, the philly, the joint, the pipe, the 40,'* and saying, *'man I have got to go home and study, I am college material.'* Sometimes about five seconds is all we have between saying, *'here is my number call me after 7PM,'* and saying, *'what would your wife say if she knew you were asking me for my phone number?'*

Sometimes, about five seconds is all we have between asking, *'did he or she really commit that terrible act? Well, let me tell you what else I know about them,'* and saying, *'they may not be perfect, but then neither am I. I am really not interested in hearing the gossip you want to pass my way.'* Sometimes about five seconds is all we have between saying, *'I hate you, and I am never going to forgive you for what you did to me. I am going to carry it around like a cancer growing inside of me,'* and saying, *'what you meant for evil God meant for good. I love you and there is not a thing you can do about it.'*

Sometimes about five seconds is all we have between self-destructing, and setting ourselves up to accomplish through God what seems impossible. Five seconds may not seem like very long. But when you are making the critical decisions that make or break a life, five seconds can mean everything.

Nothing Shall be Impossible with God

I believe if the apostle Paul were around to have seen Mission Impossible, he would have enjoyed it as much as I did. The apostle Paul knew about accomplishing the impossible through God. They told him the Gentiles could not be saved and would not accept Christ, but through God he saw it happen. They threw him in prison and beat him, and thought that would stop the spread of the Word, but the Word spread even more. Once, when he was on a ship and a storm came, all his ship mates thought they were going to die. They wanted to blame the storm on him, but he told them not one of them would lose their life. Even after the ship was wrecked they all made it safely to shore. Paul knew about accomplishing the impossible through God. He was able to say with boldness *"I can do all things through Christ which strengthens me."* (Philippians 4:13)

Do you know about accomplishing the impossible through God? Have you heard people say a lot of things down through the years but seen the hand of God unfold the impossible in your life? Have people told you what you couldn't do? Have you had to listen to a chorus of naysayers and doubters who tried to poison your dreams with their fears by telling you what couldn't be done? Is your testimony despite what those people said, God has allowed you to accomplish some things that surprised them and you?

Paul knew about the setbacks the enemy uses to prevent us from achieving what God is speaking into our lives. In this 7th Chapter of his letter to the Romans, Paul speaks honestly and candidly about one of the most effective weapons the enemy has, *the spirit of self-destruction.* This weapon is so effective because like the tape that was programmed to self-destruct after five seconds, the enemy has an explosive device called sin already inside of us. He does not have to put it there he just has to activate it. We are already programmed to do it. The enemy just has to activate what is there and it will happen naturally.

You Are Not Your Own Worst Enemy!

Sometimes I feel like I am my own worst enemy. Regardless of what I tell my friends, family, or any nosy people who inquire in my business. There are times in my life, when my failure is my own fault. It is not about what anybody else did to me, said about me, prevented me from doing, or made me do. Nobody held a gun to my head and made me do anything. If I am honest with myself, sometimes the predicament, the jam, the uncomfortable place, the situation that I find myself in is nobody else's fault but my own. Do you ever feel that way? Do you ever feel as though you have sabotaged your own success? The book of Proverbs speaks about the danger of going along with wicked people or wicked advice and it concludes that the problem is "they ambush their own lives." (Proverbs 1:18) There have been many days when I have felt just that way, like I have ambushed my own life. Have you ever been there? Sometimes I really want to admit that I shot my own self in the foot. I dropped my own candy in the dirt. Some of us feel like we are our own worst enemy sometimes.

Expose Your Real Worst Enemy!

This is exactly how your real worst enemy, the devil, wants you to feel. Our enemy, the devil, wants us to feel like we are our own worst enemy. Once we have identified who our enemy is, we can turn our efforts on destroying our enemy. If I believe I am my own worst enemy, my real enemy does not have to waste time or energy destroying me. I will do a better job destroying me than my enemy ever would. I know my weaknesses, and what has the potential to mess me up. The reason the devil wants to destroy you is to prevent, hinder, stop, detour, or distract you from becoming closer to God and becoming who you are in God. Your real worst enemy is the devil, and he knows as long as you suffer from a *self-destructive spirit* it will steal life from you. The Bible says, "we are more than conquerors through Him who loved us." (Romans 8:37) Anything the devil can do to cause us to participate in our own demise makes his job easier.

The Good News is you are not your worst enemy. No matter what you have done along the way, you are not your worst enemy. It does not matter how many bad mistakes, stupid decisions, or just plain dumb things you have done, you are not your own worst enemy. Perhaps you have done the same thing over, and over, and over again. You knew better and said you would do better, but you didn't. You still are not your own worst enemy. What you have is a self–destructive spirit attacking your spirit. The sooner you stop working against yourself, the sooner you can turn your attention on your real enemy, Satan. The sooner you get it planted in your spirit you are not your own worst enemy, the sooner you can take back your life. Establish it in your spirit today that you are not your own worst enemy. Stop saying that about yourself. Repeat after me, I am more than a conqueror through Christ who loves me. I cancel the devil's assignment in my life. I know who my real worst enemy is and I have the victory in Jesus name!

Every hurting parent needs to know that your son or daughter does not have a death wish. Every hurting wife, husband, family member, or concerned friend of some person who is spiraling down a path of self - destruction needs to know, that person does not want to end up in jail, the cemetery, or living in the streets. What that person wants more than anything is to be free from the *spirit of self- destruction.*

Maybe you know about the spirit of self-destruction. You know what it is to sabotage your own future. You know what it is to throw away a good opportunity, a good marriage, a good relationship, or good career. It was not because of racism, sexism, discrimination or mean people, but because you feel like something inside of you is broken. I have met many people in my years as a pastor who felt like something inside of them was broken. Often they could not articulate that feeling in words but the feeling was real. Most of us have experienced the feeling of inner brokenness at some point in our life. Whether it was due to the loss of a loved one, the end of a relationship, or the failure to achieve a goal, we have all been there. Take back your life by exposing your real worst enemy for whom and what he really is, *the father of lies.* (John 8:44)

Jesus encountered a father whose son was under the influence of a self-destructive spirit. It was actually a deaf and dumb spirit that caused him to do self-destructive things like throwing himself into the fire and into the water trying to die. The father asked for Jesus' help. Jesus answered, "if you can believe, all

41

things are possible to him who believes." (Mark 9:23) The father replied to Jesus that he did believe but he needed help with his unbelief. He was saying, *'Jesus I believe but I am not sure that my faith in God is strong enough.'* Even though he didn't think his faith in God was enough, it was enough for Jesus to work. Jesus commanded the spirit to come out of his son, and it did. Just think about those powerful words for one second. "All things are possible to him who believes." All things covers a multitude of sins, problems and issues. All things means no matter how bad it has been or how difficult it looks like it is going to be, supernatural help is released by believing in the power of God.

You may have been on drugs, you may have been in the streets, you may have gotten yourself into one abusive relationship after another and maybe you still are. But if you can believe in the power of God, all things are possible to those who believe. Receive that into your spirit and activate what faith in God you have to experience a miracle. Jesus was telling that father to expose that self-destructive spirit in his son to his faith. Take back your life by unleashing your faith to believe that God and God alone can give you victory over that self-destructive spirit. Unleash is the exact word I mean to use. Stop keeping your faith on a leash chained up like a dog that can't get free. Turn your faith loose on your situation and let it take a bite out of your self - destructive spirit. Unleash your faith and watch what God will do.

Recognizing the Spirit of Self-Destruction

Paul puts it this way, *"when I would do good, the good that I would do I do not do but the evil that I would not do, that I do."* (Romans 7:14) Paul is speaking about his own personal inner conflict in which there are times in his life when he feels as though he is not in control of his actions. He knows better. He knows what he is doing. He knows that what he is doing is not right. He knows it will ultimately be detrimental to him. Paul knows better, and Paul knows what he should not be doing. In fact, Paul does not even really desire to do it. But, Paul says, *'if I can just be honest, sometimes, I do it any way. I do it even though it is not in my own best interest. I do it even though it is not to my benefit. I do it even though I will probably be the one that has to pay dire consequences.'* Why? *'The spirit of self-destruction that is in me already as sin pushes me and pulls me to do the things that I have no business doing even when they are to my own self demise.'*

In order to take authority over the spirit of self-destruction in our lives, we first have to recognize that the ability to do self-destructive behavior is in us. What Paul is dealing with in Chapter Seven of Romans is not something that the devil puts on us; it is something that is in us. Its origin is Satan. Satan in the Garden of Eden tempted Eve and then Adam, who disobeyed God and engaged in their own self-destructive behavior. Their disobedience to God led them to be banished from the garden. (Genesis 3) Think about how self-destructive their behavior was in the garden. They were in the Garden of Eden. They had everything they needed, and everything they could have wanted. They allowed Satan to trick them into disobeying God. As a consequence they were booted out of Paradise and we received sin as part of our human nature. (Romans 5:12) Paul says, "What I find then is this, when I want to do good evil is also right there present with me."

(Romans 7:21) In other words the capacity for self-destructive behavior is in me no matter who I am, because sin was born into my nature.

David describes our predicament this way in Psalm 51:5, we are "born in sin and shaped in iniquity." Certainly David is qualified to talk about having a self-destructive spirit because he too wrestled with his own willingness to do what displeased God. I choose to describe it with the wise words of a musical genius named George Clinton, *"why must I be like that, why must I chase the cat, it's nothin but the dog in me."*

The dangerous person is not the person who recognizes they are capable of self-destructive behavior, and acknowledges it. That person will ask God to help them to overcome the *spirit of self-destruction.* The dangerous person is the one who tries to act like self-destructive behavior is beyond them and says, *'I'm just holy, I'm just perfect, and I am just pure. I am alright, I am fine, and I will be okay.'* That person is dangerous because they are only fooling themselves, and the enemy is just waiting to activate what is already inside of us. I Corinthians 10:12 issues a serious warning to all of those who unwisely count themselves among the *spiritually arrived,* "Therefore let him who thinks he stands take heed lest he falls." Take back your life by admitting you are not strong enough to overcome the *spirit of self – destruction* by yourself. Ask our Father to help you and watch what will happen.

Don't Get Trigger Happy

There are some diseases, such as sickle cell anemia in which a person may not have the disease, but they can be a carrier of the trait. If they are a carrier of the trait they have to be careful about whom they marry, or have children with. If they hook up with another person who is a carrier, they can pass on to the child what neither of them has but both of them carry. If you know the enemy will try to get you to engage in self-destructive behavior in a particular way, don't spend all of your time around people who have the same weaknesses. I may not be engaging in self-destructive behaviors right at this point in my life, but if I am a carrier I can still be dangerous if connected with another carrier. If I like to gossip, I shouldn't hang around gossips. If I like to sleep around, I shouldn't hang around at the *players club*. If I like to use substances, I shouldn't hang around people who are using those substances. If I like to make quick money, I should not hang around drug dealers or quick scam artists. I don't want what is already there to be activated in my life. In the world of therapy they call these kinds of influences triggers. Triggers are simply influences, people, or situations that trigger our engagement in self -destructive behavior. The book of James says that "each one is tempted when he is carried away by his own lust." (James 1:14) That simply means that there is something on the inside of us that is a trigger to self-destructive behavior. That something is sin. Take back your life by taking your finger off the trigger. Don't pull the trigger!

You Got Yours & I Got Mine!

We take authority over the *spirit of self-destruction* by realizing not all self-destructive behavior is the same. How can I take authority over something I have not even identified as a problem? While jealousy, which we will talk about next, is a master of disguise, self- destruction is a sneak. Notice what Paul does in this passage of scripture. He is very careful not to name any specific behaviors. All he says is, "the evil that I don't want to do, that is what I end up doing." He does not tell us what evil he is talking about. He does not provide us with examples of the types of things that he struggles with. All he says is, "the evil that I don't want to do, I end up doing." One of the things the absence of examples suggests to us is we should not be so quick to categorize different behaviors as self-destructive or exclude them from our list of self-destructive behaviors. I don't have to abuse my body to be self-destructive. I don't have to waste my life to be self-destructive. You don't have to do some self-mutilation or self-inflicted pain to be self-destructive. All you have to do is keep on sinning. Sin is self-destructive in any form because sin is what delays us from becoming who we are in God. Delay is not a strong enough word. Sin is what separates us from God. There is a saying you may have heard: "life is short, death is sure, sin is the cause, and Christ is the cure." There is no point in acting like we are better than anybody else, because sin is self -destructive behavior, and the Bible reminds us that "all have sinned and fall short of the glory of God." (Romans 3:23)

Take Authority Over Self Destruction!

How then, do we take authority over the spirit of self-destruction? I am sure by now you have several questions about how to take back your life from the *spirit of self-destruction*. You may be asking, *'Pastor, I hear you. You have told me in order to take authority over the spirit of self-destruction in my life I have to recognize there is some behavior going on in my life that is self-destructive*

You have also told me I have to realize I do have the capacity to be self-destructive within me, because of our sinful nature. I need to recognize we all have the capacity to allow the spirit of self-destruction to be active in our lives.

But Pastor, I still don't feel I have the tools to take real authority over the spirit of self-destruction in my life. I want my life back and I am not sure how to take it back from self-destruction just yet. More than that Pastor, I have someone in my life who is suffering from a spirit of self-destruction right now, and I still don't feel as though I know what to do to help them take authority over that spirit in their life.'

Your questions are valid and real. This passage of Scripture from Paul would be one depressing passage if it were not for what Paul says in verses 24-25. After wrestling with the issue of the *spirit of self-destruction* and experiencing frustrations similar to ours, Paul comes to the same conclusion we do. What am I supposed to do about the *spirit of self-destruction* when the enemy tries to bring it out in my life? But in verses 24-25 he gives the answer. He says, "O wretched man that I am! Who will deliver me from this body of death? I thank God - through Jesus Christ our Lord." (Romans 7:24-25) What Paul concludes is we don't have what it takes to take authority over the *spirit of self-destruction*. I repeat, if we could save ourselves from the spirit of *self-destruction* by our own devices we would have a long time ago. We cannot. The only way to take authority over the *spirit of self-destruction* is for Jesus to take authority over you. We take authority over the *spirit of self-destruction* when we let

Jesus take authority over us.

Paul concludes he is weak, imperfect, and sinful by nature. You can if you choose to but I am not leaving Paul out there by himself. He has at least one classmate; I am also weak, imperfect and sinful by nature. I don't always do what I am supposed to do, and have frequently done what I had no business doing. Left to his own devices, Paul says he will always do what takes him further away from his divine purpose. But, Paul says, '*I am turning my life over to Jesus. Where I am weak Jesus will make me strong. Where I fall short, Jesus will pick me up. Where I am tempted to mess up, Jesus will show up in my life.*'

Take authority over self-destruction by giving Jesus authority in your life. Take back your life by surrendering it to Jesus. We love to sing in church about surrendering all to Jesus, but when we say all; most of us mean all of our problems. What we must surrender to Jesus is our lives, our mind, our will, our emotions, in other words, our souls. "For whoever wishes to save his life will lose it, but whoever loses his life for My sake, he is the one who will save it." (Luke 9:24)

I May Not Know How, But I Do Know Who!

Sometimes on Sundays when people join our church I tell them that people don't have a problem getting saved. Nobody wants to die and spend eternity in Hell. The problem is Jesus wants to occupy first place in our life. Jesus wants to sit on the throne in our life, and if you give your life to Jesus, He will take authority over every demon that tries to cause you to engage in self-destructive behavior. Paul was educated, well trained, and scholarly. He was well acquainted with the great theories and philosophies of his day. But when it comes down to this matter of self-destructive behavior, Paul's final answer is none of those theories or philosophies can fix me, but Jesus can.

When I pastored in New Orleans, Louisiana, one year we were having Vacation Bible School, and I went into the social hall to check on the junior classes. I was pleased when I saw the small children writing Dear Jesus letters. Some wrote, "Dear Jesus, I love You because You died for me." Others wrote, "Dear Jesus, I love You because You gave me my parents." Some wrote, "Dear Jesus, I love You because You answered my prayers." But there was one letter that has forever remained in my memory. One little student's letter summed it up for me in a way that blessed my spirit. She simply wrote, "Dear Jesus I love You because there are some things I can't do, that only You can do."

That little girl got it right. There are some things we cannot do that only Jesus can do. I am not too sophisticated to say Jesus fixed me one day. I tried drugs, but drugs couldn't fix me. I tried alcohol, but alcohol couldn't fix me. I tried the psychologists but the psychologist couldn't fix me. I tried what my friends had to say, but my friends couldn't fix me. One day I tried Jesus, and I found out that my little student was correct; there are some things we can't do that only Jesus can do.

The answer to taking authority over the *spirit of self-destruction* is not a how answer. There are no methods, techniques, or disciplines that can guarantee we will not slip at a moments' notice. The answer is a not a how answer because when it comes to the *spirit of self-destruction* the answer is Who. Paul asks the most important question of all as he wrestles with the *spirit of self-destruction* in his own life. His question is not how do I get rid of this spirit? His question is "Who shall deliver me from this body of death?" Paul never did come up with an answer to the how to deal with the *spirit of self- destruction*, but he serves as a constant reminder to us that even when we do not know how, as long as we have Jesus in our lives, we do know Who.

Pardon me a moment while I praise Him! I may not know how, but I know Who! I may not have a methodology or technique, but I know Who! I may not have it all figured out and worked out, but I know Who! If you have not met the Who that will cause you to take back your life from the *spirit of self-destruction*, His Name is Jesus! There is power in His Name! There is healing in His Name! There is deliverance in His Name! There is victory in His Name! There is overcoming in His Name! There is forgiveness in His Name! "At the Name of Jesus every knee shall bow... and every tongue shall confess that Christ is Lord to the glory of God the Father." (Philippians 2:10-11)

Prayer: Lord God in the Name of Jesus I come before You admitting that sometimes I have a self-destructive spirit. I have no excuse for why I have done some of the things I have done. You told me in Your Word that Your eyes are always upon me and You see the good, the bad and the ugly. I don't know why You love me the way You do. Thank You for Your grace, mercy, and forgiveness. I confess that I am not strong enough to overcome the demonic influence of a self-destructive spirit by myself. But You promised in Your

Word that You would never leave me nor forsake me. Deliver me today! I receive it in Jesus Name. Amen!

Chapter Four

The Spirit of Jealousy!

"So I sent messengers to them saying, "I am doing a great work, and I cannot come down. Why should the work cease while I leave it and go down to you?" Nehemiah 6:3 (NKJV)

While you may be excited about your decision to take back your life, please know that the devil is not happy. The devil will use fear, doubt, and self-destruction to try to steal life from you. John 10:10 says that he comes to "steal, kill, and destroy." In other words, he only shows up with bad intentions. If none of his previous methods are having their desired effect, he will resort to the *spirit of jealousy* to try to take you off course from your God appointed destiny.

One afternoon while preparing to teach my Bible class a verse of Scripture jumped out at me like never before. It was in John chapter 3. John the Baptist was baptizing people in a place called Aenon. His followers came to him and told him that Jesus, whom he had baptized on the other side of the Jordan River, was now baptizing people. In fact, they said, everybody is now coming to Him to be baptized. (John 3:26) Can't you just see that scene playing out? John's followers probably thought they were protecting him by letting him know Jesus was now drawing big crowds for baptism. They expected John to react in the same way as they were reacting. They expected him to become jealous and to say, 'who does that Jesus think He is?' But John gives an answer that shows he really was a man sent from God. John says, "A man can receive nothing, unless it has been given him from heaven." (John 3:27) In other words, John says that whatever honor or blessings come to any of us originate in heaven, and if they don't originate in heaven then they aren't worth having.

Sometimes in Christian circles we use catch phrases and buzz words that may or may not line up with God's Word. You have heard them before, phrases like, *God is good all the time, and all the time God is good.* Sometimes they are based on songs, Christian experiences, or legends of the church. One that is based on a song says, *what God has for me is for me.* John's answer to his followers in John 3:27 is a biblical basis for that saying. They expected jealousy from John the Baptist, but what they experienced was trust in the providence of God. That does not prevent the enemy from trying to use the *spirit of jealousy* every time he can. Satan recognizes jealousy as a powerful tool that steals life from us. It distracts us from our purpose. He tried to make John jealous of Jesus, but he was unsuccessful because John understood who he was. John also knew what he did, and did not, have control over.

You don't have any control over who God blesses. Thank the Lord nobody else has any control over when, how much, or how often God blesses you. Psalm 75 reminds us "promotion is not from the east or the west, but it is God who judges." Take back your life by celebrating instead of hating the blessings, and anointing of God in the lives of others.

The Book of Nehemiah contains one of the most powerful stories in the Bible. It is an historical work recounting the struggles of a man named Nehemiah as he tries to help his people rebuild their city after destruction and defeat. Nehemiah was living well and doing well for himself. He had risen to the rank of cup bearer to the king of Persia. He enjoyed a comfortable life and lived in the palace. Nehemiah is informed that his people, the Jews, are doing poorly and their cities have been destroyed and their spirit broken. As a result his heart is heavy and he knows he must do something to improve the situation. Despite his personal good fortune Nehemiah does not have the *"I got mine and later for everybody else mentality."* He feels a sense of responsibility for the people and the place from which he came. Nehemiah prays and asks God for guidance and finally decides he must return to help his people rebuild. It could not have been an easy decision for Nehemiah to make but it was a prayerful decision which gave him confidence he was following the direction of God for his life.

Everybody Won't Celebrate Your Blessings!

Guess what? Nehemiah is coming back home and he is going to help us rebuild. Don't you just know everyone is going to be glad to see Nehemiah, and welcome him back to be part of the rebuilding process? Not quite. Everybody is not happy and excited that Nehemiah has come back to help rebuild the wall. Some people ask, *'Who does Nehemiah think he is our savior?'* Others say, *'Who told Nehemiah we needed him to come back here and help us?'* Some people are saying, *'Oh yeah Mr. Billy Bad Nehemiah; well I would like to see you try.'* Others are just plain old jealous.

You Ain't the First Nor the Last!

Since the dawn of humanity people have been jealous of one another. The Bible says Adam and Eve initially had two sons, Cain and Abel. Cain was jealous that God accepted Abel's sacrifice, but refused his and became the murderer of his brother. Not too much later the Bible tells us Jacob had twelve sons, but some of the sons were jealous of their brother Joseph. They were so jealous in fact they threw their own brother in a pit and sold him into slavery. If we were to journey throughout the Bible we would find it was jealousy that caused Saul to try to take David's life. It was jealousy that helped to drive a wedge between David and his son Absalom. It was jealousy that caused the other government officials in Babylon to make accusations against Daniel. Ultimately, it was jealousy that propelled Judas into being the betrayer of Jesus. You remember what happened when Judas saw the woman anoint Jesus feet with expensive perfume. "Why did you let that woman waste that expensive oil on your feet Jesus? Don't you know how many poor people we could have fed with that?" (John 12:5)

Some spirits cause detours to our destiny but jealousy is much more sinister. Jealousy is a spirit that can ruin our lives, and the lives of others. If the *spirit of jealousy* gets on us, we have to be careful, because jealousy makes us dangerous to ourselves, and dangerous to others. Jealousy is a two edge sword that can cause us to do harm to ourselves and to someone else.

Change Triggers Jealousy!

In Nehemiah, the Bible does not explicitly describe the actions of those persons who were angry at Nehemiah as being jealous. However, we recognize jealousy when we see it. There was a man named Sanballat who was a Samaritan, and he was not particularly fond of the Jews. Sanballat was a big person around there in Israel in the aftermath of the exile. He had a little crowd of people who looked up to him, and perhaps came to him for advice. They felt important by being around him. It did not seem to matter to Sanballat that the city was in ruins, as long as he was comfortable. There are always those who can disregard how pitiful the situation is as long as they are comfortable and can feel like a big person. The walls were falling down but he was comfortable. The people were hurting and in need but he was comfortable. The people had lost their spirit, their will to succeed, and their drive to even rebuild for themselves but Sanballat was comfortable. As a matter of fact as a hater of the Jews he was quite comfortable with them appearing disheartened and weakened. Do you know what made Sanballat uncomfortable? Nehemiah made him very uncomfortable.

Sadly we have some Sanballats in churches today. Nobody is getting saved, but I'm comfortable. No lives are being transformed, but I'm comfortable. The church can be experiencing a famine of spiritual, numerical, and financial growth, but I'm comfortable. So please don't bother the music. Please don't start changing things around. For God's sake please don't start trying to rebuild any walls in here. If you do, I might just be uncomfortable. Do you know what made Sanballat uncomfortable? He was uncomfortable when Nehemiah came back and started to rebuild the walls of Jerusalem.

The Bible says that Sanballat along with his two flunkies, Tobiah and Geshem were upset when they heard Nehemiah had started to rebuild the wall. As a matter of fact it says they were very wroth or very angry. Do you know why they were angry? They were angry, because they had been overtaken by the *spirit of jealousy*. Anger is just one of the manifestations of a jealous spirit. The *spirit of jealousy* will cause us to hate those we love because we see them being blessed. The *spirit of jealousy* will cause us to bad mouth people we don't even know because they are doing something we never even thought about doing. The *spirit of jealousy* will cause us to be used by our enemy for his purposes and his plan, to our own detriment. Proverbs 27:4 says, "wrath is fierce and anger is a flood, But who can stand against jealousy?" They were jealous of Nehemiah because Nehemiah was doing something they weren't. They were jealous because Nehemiah would be celebrated for his efforts and in their own small minds they would be forgotten. Nehemiah had been given a vision from God that was bigger than they could imagine, and he was acting on it. People may not always become jealous of you just because you have a big vision but you can always expect jealousy when you begin to act upon a God given vision.

The Danger of Jealousy!

What is the *spirit of jealousy*? It is a tool of our enemy, Satan that is used to destroy us from the inside out. It is a weapon the devil uses to break up friendships, and destroy relationships. It is a life stealer because it makes big people small and strong people weak. Sanballat, Tobiah, and Geshem, had been there in the city for years and they knew the condition of the people, and of the walls of the city. They were well acquainted with how devastating the invasions of the Persian armies and others had been on the people of Jerusalem, but they had done nothing about it. It was not their place to do anything about the situation of the Jews because they were not Jews. Neither was it their place to try to prevent Nehemiah from achieving his vision.

Have you ever wondered why people who have nothing to do with you want to know everything about you? How do people who have nothing to do with you have plenty to say about how you carry out the vision that God has given you for your life? Nehemiah was not trying to make any enemies or to upset the apple cart. He was not trying to make people angry at him. He was simply walking in the anointing God had given him to rebuild the walls of the city. Yet Sanballat, Tobiah, and Geshem were jealous of him.

Perhaps, if Nehemiah had gone back to rebuild just any old city it might have been more acceptable but Nehemiah had gone back to rebuild Jerusalem. Jerusalem was the center of religious faith and practice for the Jewish people. Jerusalem was the city that David had to take men and go up through the gutters and the sewer system to be able to take for the Lord. (2 Samuel 5:8) Jerusalem was where the temple had been a national shrine and place of pilgrimage for Jews everywhere. Jerusalem held a special place in the life of the Jewish people. So much so that even after the exile the people lamented in the 137th Psalm "by the rivers of Babylon, there we sat down, yea, we wept, when we remembered Zion." Jerusalem was special because it was the *city of David, the city on a hill*. When Nehemiah said he was going back to rebuild Jerusalem, it was an act of worship. It was a spiritual offering unto God. So the enemy couldn't just sit still and let him do that good work without any trouble.

When you commit yourself to an assignment God places in your heart such as rebuilding your life, or rebuilding the lives of others as a sacrifice to God, the enemy will try to use his whole arsenal to stop you from completing your assignment. Take back your life by renewing your commitment to the assignment God deposited in your heart and defeating the *spirit of jealousy* when it shows up. If you take the first three letters off of jealousy you find out exactly what jealousy is all about. It is a lousy spirit that steals life.

The enemy puts a *spirit of jealousy* on Sanballat, Tobiah, and Geshem. This story is not about Sanballat, Tobiah, and Geshem. It is it really not even about Nehemiah. It is about God using Nehemiah to rebuild the holy city, and the enemy using Sanballat, Tobiah, and Geshem to try to stop Him. God uses people and so does the devil. Which one are you, God's tool, or the devil's fool? Don't be a pawn in the game by allowing the enemy to make you jealous about what God is doing through someone else's life. On a chess board there are more pawns than anything else. Pawns are the weakest players on the board and the most expendable. Ironically, only a pawn which makes it all the way to the other end of the board can also become a queen, the most powerful player on the board. Don't let the devil use you as his pawn by making you jealous of others. Reverse his plan, take back your power, and take back your life. When Sanballat, Tobiah, and Geshem showed up, they did not admit that they were jealous. Perhaps they didn't even realize it themselves. They showed up to the work site, and instead of bringing their hard hats and hammers, they brought criticism and ridicule. They even conspired with others and planned how they could interrupt the work that

Nehemiah was doing.

Jealousy is a Master of Disguise

The spirit of jealousy rarely shows up dressed as what it really is. Jealousy is a master of disguise.   It shows up as concern. *'Oh, I'm just concerned about this thing that's all.'*   It shows up as anger, *'they offended me and they should not have done that, in that way.'* Look at what Judas says to Jesus. He does not ask, *'why couldn't she put some perfume on my feet too?'* He doesn't say, *'That foot massage sure must feel good, I think I would like to have that kind of treatment.'*   He asks, 'Why are we wasting that expensive perfume on your feet when we could be feeding a lot of poor people with the money from that perfume?' (John 12) The *spirit of jealousy* has attacked him, but it does not come out as jealousy, it comes out as concern for the poor. Judas is not only jealous, he is also a thief. It is easy for a jealous person to be a thief, because to be jealous is to covet, which is to want what someone else has.

Often, we don't even realize what it is we are dealing with until we get so close up on it that it has the opportunity to destroy us. When the *spirit of jealousy* gets on us, we don't think we are jealous. We don't believe we are being used by the enemy to work against Gods' plan. We honestly and sincerely think we are right.   We have to ask ourselves when we find ourselves offended at this person, angry at that person, not speaking to another person, gossiping about the next person, and speaking negative thoughts into the spirit of another person, what is really going on here with me? Has a *spirit of jealousy* over taken me and caused me to behave in such a way in which God is not pleased? The *spirit of jealousy* disguises itself so we often don't recognize what is really going on until it is too late. Take back your life by recognizing jealousy rarely shows up dressed as plain old jealousy. It comes to the party of your life dressed in a costume. It hides behind a mask of anger, concern, or offense.

Jealousy is a High Stakes Player

The spirit of jealousy also shows up when the stakes are high. Nehemiah has left his home in the palace as the cupbearer to the king to come back to rebuild the city of God. Let's forget about what the rebuilding of the city meant for one minute, and just consider what an impact that had to have on people to see someone with that type of faith commitment. Just imagine how that must have impacted people to see someone who loved God enough to give himself to the work of the Lord in such a way. When I say the stakes are high, I am not talking about what we consider to be high stakes, or what we consider to be important things. I am talking about when God considers the stakes to be high. Whenever you are doing something important to God, you had better expect the *spirit of jealousy* to be somewhere around. Whenever you are doing something major in the eyes of God, you had better expect the enemy to use his spirit weapons to try to undo what God is doing. Why would anybody be jealous of you, when you are just a single parent trying to raise your kids and do the best you can? What you may not realize is that those children you are raising are God's precious possession. You don't know who you are raising that God is going to use to do His work at some future date. You may feel like you don't have anything for anybody to be jealous about. You don't need to have anything for the enemy to use jealousy as a weapon against you, just try to do something to the glory of God.

The enemy doesn't care about what you have. The enemy is not worried about your having possessions. In fact, the enemy will give you possessions. Isn't that what he told Jesus out in the wilderness? In Luke 4:6, "I will give you the world and everything in it." You can have all of the *stuff* in the world. The devil neither wants, nor needs, your car, your house, or your designer clothes. The enemy is not worried about the *stuff* you have. The enemy is worried about the *stuff* you do. Anytime you try to do something to the glory of God, even if it is just raising your children by yourself, it attracts the devil's attention. If you are doing it to the glory of God, the enemy will try to steal life from you.

They were not worried about Nehemiah while he was living in the palace as the cup bearer to the king. The devil was not attacking him while he was living in palace luxury. He had plenty of *stuff, while* living in the palace. Nehemiah became a problem when he started doing something to the glory of God. So when the stakes are high look for the *spirit of jealousy* to be present. Take back your life by realizing you are not defined by your *stuff.* You are defined by your obedience to the assignment God has given you. Whether you have all the *stuff* in the world or none of the *stuff* in the world, you become a problem for the enemy when you decide to take back your life by doing what God has assigned you to do.

Jealousy Interrupts Assignments!

Jealousy always comes as an interruption to what you are trying to accomplish. Nehemiah is not bothering anybody. He is minding his business rebuilding the wall. He and the people are at peace and working together and here come Sanballat, Tobiah, and Geshem. They say, *'Nehemiah, Nehemiah, come down here and meet us at the plain of Ono. We need to talk to you'.* But Nehemiah tells them I'm sorry but I am busy. So they call again, *'Nehemiah, Nehemiah, come down and meet with us at Ono'.* I always like to say that Ono really means Oh No you don't think you are about to accomplish that goal. Oh No you don't believe that God is going to bless you anyhow. Oh No you don't think that if you hold on to Jesus, despite all of your troubles, that the Lord will make a way somehow.

Have you ever received an invitation to Ono? Have you ever received an invitation to oh no you can't, oh no you won't, and oh no you are not big enough, strong enough, or faithful enough? Have you ever been invited to Ono? When you receive an invitation to Ono, don't RSVP. Don't call and confirm. Don't check your schedule to see if you are available. If you want to take authority over the *spirit of jealousy,* just do what Nehemiah did when he was invited to Ono. Nehemiah said I have received your invitation to Ono, but I'm sorry, "I am doing a great work and I can't come down to meet with you." (Nehemiah 6:3) Nehemiah recognized the importance of the work that he was doing. He describes it as a great work. Sometimes jealousy can become a distraction to us when we don't realize the importance of what God has assigned us to do.

Not only did Nehemiah refuse to stop working and come down and meet, but Nehemiah asked God to give him the strength to continue the work. His prayer which can be found in Nehemiah 6:9 was simple and to the point, "now, therefore, O God, strengthen my hands." There are many powerful and anointed prayers in the Bible. Although the prayer of Nehemiah is simple and short, it is meaningful to anyone who is under attack. "O God, strengthen my hands." Responding to a jealous spirit at work against you can be spiritually, emotionally, and mentally draining. Don't try to rely on your own strength and power to overcome that spirit. Pray the prayer of Nehemiah and experience the supernatural resolve that comes from asking God to strengthen your hands.

The *spirit of jealousy* craves, needs, and thrives on a response. When we respond to the *spirit of jealousy* we feed it so that it grows even bigger. Tell the *spirit of jealousy* I'm sorry, I am doing a great work and I can't come down. I can't come down to deal with pettiness. I can't come down to deal with he said - she said, and I can't come down to deal with gossip. Why should the work cease while I come down to Ono and meet with you? Doing great work sparks the fire of jealousy, but remaining focused and committed to great work puts the fire out. Many people are distracted from their assignment because they become preoccupied with who is jealous of them. They are always worried about who does not like them, and who is saying mean things about them. They stop working on the wall that God has assigned them to build and come down to the plain of Oh No. Take back your life by refusing to make jealousy, in whatever form it shows up, the focus of your life.

Prayer: Lord in the name of Jesus I cancel the *spirit of jealousy* in my life. Lord make me aware when I am jealous of others and help me to focus on what You have anointed me to do rather than on what You have anointed others to do. I ask for discernment to recognize when jealousy is disguising itself as something else. Make me recognize when I am on an assignment from You and jealousy is inviting me to Oh No. Keep me focused Lord to pray the prayer of Nehemiah, Lord strengthen my hands. In Jesus Name. Amen!

Chapter Five

The Spirit of Self-Righteousness!

"I tell you, this man went down to his house justified rather than the other; for everyone who exalts himself shall be humbled, but he who humbles himself shall be exalted."
Luke 18:14 (NASB)

It is entirely possible for us to be absolutely right and absolutely wrong both at the same time. Have you ever been in one of those situations when you were right but you were wrong at the same time? You were right about what you were saying, but wrong how you said it! You were right about what you were doing, but wrong how you did it! You knew your friend did not look good in that outfit, but they really wanted it. The minute you heard the words come out of your mouth, you knew that you should not have said them. You knew that person did not presently have the skills that were necessary to accomplish their dream, but it was their dream and the minute you said those words you saw something die in them. Has anyone ever said something to you that was absolutely right, but hurt so deeply you could not even focus on the rightness of their words? Do you know what it is to be right but to still feel empty? You can be right and still feel as though you have lost. It is entirely possible to be right but to be incomplete! We take back our lives from the enemy when we realize there is more to life than just being right.

Several years ago, my wife and I were on our way into the movie theatre. On our way up the escalator we saw a man whose wife we also knew. While we were going up the escalator, he was coming down the escalator, and he was holding hands coming out of the movies, with a woman who was not his wife. He acted as though he didn't see us, and we acted as though we didn't see him. *'Well, Pastor, maybe you didn't see what you thought you saw, you don't know who that woman was.'* You are absolutely correct.

Neither my wife nor I ever said a word to his wife about that day because as right as we may have called ourselves by telling that woman what we thought we saw, we did not believe that it would have been right. Sometimes we do more damage to people in the name of being right, than we can even imagine. It is dangerous to invest ourselves too much in the idea of being right and too little in the value of being right with God.

Our enemy, Satan, uses spirits to hinder us from becoming who we are in God. Some of those spirits, such as fear and doubt are harmful to us. Others, such as jealousy, are even more dangerous because they have the potential to make us not only harmful to ourselves, but also harmful to others. Some of those spirits, such as self-destruction, are so horrible because in order to use them Satan only has to activate the sin that is already part of our human nature. We do Satan's work of destroying ourselves for him. There is, however, another spirit that our enemy uses that is especially harmful, and especially effective on Christians, the *spirit of self-righteousness.*

Righteous vs. Unrighteous

What is self-righteousness? Let's answer that question in reverse. To be righteous is to be morally upright, virtuous or godly. It is to live in accordance with the standards that God has set for us as believers.

God does expect us to try our best to live righteous lives. We could study for one whole year all the Bible tells us about being righteous. The Bible, God's Holy Word, tells us God is righteous. It tells us, many are the afflictions of the righteous. It tells us, little in the hand of a righteous person is more than much in the hand of an unrighteous person. David in his latter days tells us, he once was young, but now he is old, but he has never seen the righteous forsaken, nor their seed begging bread. James tells us, the effectual fervent prayers of the righteous avail much. Solomon tells us, in the Proverbs when the righteous are in authority, the people rejoice. Isaiah tells us; our righteousness is like filthy rags before the Lord. It is always in order for us to strive towards righteousness. It is always in order for us to ask God to incline our hearts to live in accordance to His Word. God's Word reveals God's will, and way for our lives.

To be unrighteous is to live opposite to the standards God has established for our lives. It is to live as though there is no God, and to do what we know to be wrong in the eyes of God. The Bible also has much to say about unrighteousness. It tells us, there is no unrighteousness in God. It tells us, the unrighteous will not inherit the kingdom of God. The kingdom of God is described in Romans 14:17 as "righteousness, and peace, and joy in the Holy Spirit." Unrighteousness can cause us to suppress, hide or ignore the truth of God. The Bible says God turned over certain people to a depraved mind because they "suppressed the truth in unrighteousness." (Romans 1:28) In other words they knew better, they simply chose not to do better. Peter tells us, unrighteousness earns wages which is the wrath of God.

What is Self-Righteousness?

Being righteous is a good trait. It is something to strive for, to live in accordance with God's Word and God's standards for my life. Being unrighteous is something to avoid, because it means to live in opposition, or disobedience to God's Word. What does it mean to be self-righteous?

The reason the Pharisees, the group of Jewish leaders who were in such opposition to Jesus, hated Jesus so much was because time and time again Jesus exposed them for their self - righteousness. Jesus exposed the fact that, as holy and as sanctified as they appeared to be, deep down inside they were suffering from a tragic misunderstanding of what it means to be in relationship with God. This misunderstanding was catastrophic in the life of the people because it caused the Pharisees to turn more people away from God than they brought to God. Jesus view of the Pharisees could be summarized in His quote of the prophet Isaiah in Matthew 15:8, "This people honor Me with their lips, but their heart is far away from Me." (NASB)

Throughout the Gospels, Jesus and the Pharisees are at odds because everywhere Jesus goes; all kinds of people come around Jesus. Prostitutes, sinners, beggars and tax collectors, you name the sin; there was somebody around Jesus who did it. The problem with Jesus was He also went to church. So now all of a sudden you had all of these people coming to church who had not been perfect all of their lives. Some had done some dirt along the way, and some were probably still doing dirt.

Here they were walking around church when

they were not supposed to be walking, because they hadn't spent their whole life in church learning when to walk and not walk in church. Those poor Pharisees were just so distracted they could not even focus on their worship service because they were so bothered by those people. Jesus brought people to church that did not have church clothes so they just wore what they had. They wore these clothes the same way they wore them in the world. This offended the Pharisees to no end.

The Pharisees had a nice comfortable little thing going on with a handful of people and here comes Jesus. Jesus showed up at the church, and all of those hurting, needy, and imperfect people who had been following Jesus around started coming to church.

Truthfully, preachers owe an apology to our churches. We owe an apology because when we are assigned to serve as pastor of a church, one of the first things we do is to get on the prayer line, and invite Jesus to come to our church. We forget that when we invite Jesus to church, people are going to start showing up. We forget that when we invite Jesus to church, some imperfect people might show up. Some drug dealers and drug users might show up. We forget that when we invite Jesus to the church, some thugs and alcoholics might show up, and some people who are struggling with issues in their sexuality might show up. We forget that when we invite Jesus to our church, God forbid, some sinners might show up. Because whenever Jesus shows up that is who shows up too. Two sisters joined a church I was pastoring. They were straight out of the neighborhood, and two of the best members I ever had. They loved the Lord, and they loved to serve.

Sometimes on Sunday they would wear outfits that made some of the saints raise their eyebrows. I loved it! God loved those women and they loved God no matter what they had on.

What does it mean to be self-righteous? Why is the spirit of self-righteousness such an effective tool in hindering us from achieving our purpose in God? What must we, who are saved, do to take back our life from the *spirit of self-righteousness*?

Recognize Your Need for Mercy

In Luke chapter 18 Jesus gives a parable about two men. One of the men is a tax collector. Tax collectors were not popular among the Jewish people. They were working for the government that was oppressing the people. Many of them were skimming some extra off the people for themselves. That's why the Pharisees were really bothered when they saw Jesus hanging around the tax collectors. It drove them crazy when Jesus went to have dinner at the house of Zacchaeus, the tax collector, and they really must have been upset when they saw that Matthew, aka Levi; one of His best disciples was himself a former tax collector. So, here is Jesus telling a story about two men and one of them is a tax collector. We already know who we shouldn't like in this story, right?

The other man in this story is a righteous man. He happens to be a Pharisee, a member of the religious group that was always opposing Jesus. Both men go to the temple to talk to God and the Pharisee goes first. Listen to his prayer, "God I thank you that I am not like other men, robbers, evil doers, adulterers, or even like this tax collector. I fast twice a week and I give a tenth

71

The Pharisee says in effect he is trying to live a righteous life. He is trying to live in obedience to God's Word. He is tithing and he is fasting. He is faithful to his wife, and he does no evil. Is he wrong for trying to live a righteous life before God? Is he wrong for being an honest person and a good person? Is he wrong for putting God first in his life by giving God one tenth or a tithe of all his earnings? He is certainly not wrong for trying to live a righteous life before God.

Jesus goes on to say that the tax collector stood afar off from the Pharisee and he began to pray. Listen to the tax collector's prayer. "God have mercy on me, a sinner." (Luke 18:13) That's it. He says nothing about all that he has done for God. He is not under any illusion that he is doing God any favors. He is not under the assumption he is any better or any worse than anyone else. He simply states the obvious; he is a sinner in need of the Lord's mercy.

Jesus said, of the two men the tax collector was the one who went back justified before God. To be justified is to be found innocent. In other words he came and he asked for mercy and he got mercy. He got what he needed because he recognized what he needed. The Pharisee didn't get what he needed because he did not think he needed anything. Sometimes we do not get what we need from God. We don't have sense enough to know that no matter how good we think we are we still need the mercy of God. God does not love us because we are so good. God loves us because of who He is. 1 John 4:10 says, "Herein is love, not that we loved God, but that he loved us, and sent His Son to be the propitiation for our sins." Propitiation simply

72

means to make favorable or appease. It is a word that is frequently associated with God's mercy. Through the death of Jesus on the cross God has exercised mercy on us for our sins. We didn't earn it, and we certainly didn't deserve it.

There is a popular definition for grace and mercy I like to use. Grace is getting from God what we did not deserve. It is unmerited blessing. Mercy is not getting from God what we do deserve. It is God withholding from us the wrath that our actions have earned. Take back your life by recognizing that you are never so good that you escape the need for God's mercy. The Bible says that David was a man after God's own heart and still in the 23rd Psalm David rejoices that "goodness and mercy shall follow him all the days of his life." If David rejoiced over mercy, shouldn't we?

To be self-righteous is to believe that we are good all by ourselves. To be self- righteous is to believe because we are striving to be obedient to God that it makes us better than those who have not come to that understanding. It is to believe that, because we strive to live in accordance to God's Word, we are better than others. But to be self-righteous is to be blind to the tragedy of our own condition. The enemy wants to put a *spirit of self-righteousness* on us that will keep us from growing in God. The enemy wants to put a *spirit of self-righteousness* on us that will keep our churches from growing. The enemy wants to give us the *spirit of self-righteousness* so we turn people away from God instead of bringing them to God. The enemy wants to give us a *spirit of self-righteousness* so we will be blind to our own sin.

Self-Righteousness Muffles Our Testimony

If we are to take authority over the *spirit of self-righteousness* in our lives we must recognize the *spirit of self-righteousness* muffles our testimony. That is what the enemy really wants, isn't it? It is bad enough that God has done something in your life. Since the enemy cannot stop us from receiving the miracle God wants to do in our life, he wants to makes us self-righteous. That way he can prevent anyone else from being blessed by our testimony of what God has done for us. The Bible says that we overcame the accuser "because of the blood of the lamb and because of the word of our testimony." (Revelation 12:11)

The enemy steals life from us when he muffles our testimony because he understands that the words of our testimony give us and others victory over him. You did not get to where you are today by yourself. It was not because you were so cute, so smart, or had all of the right connections. If there was a right connection at all it was your connection to the true and living God; the God who hears and answers our prayers.

None of us have made it through the trials and struggles of life just because we are so wonderful. We have a testimony! Maybe you started in the projects and God put a teacher in your life who believed in you. Now you are at the top of your field. Maybe you came from a dysfunctional family but God put a hedge around you that protected you from the drama. You became the one in your neighborhood who made it out alive. Maybe you were in abusive relationships, the victim of sexual abuse, or addicted to drugs. God brought you out "clothed and in your right mind." You have a testimony.

We are thieves of God's glory when we act like we made it by ourselves. Don't forget that it was the Lord who fought your battles. Self-righteousness is dangerous because it makes us think and act like we don't have a testimony. Somebody is waiting for your testimony. Your testimony is going to help turn somebody's life around who is going through what you went through. Take back your life by refusing to allow a *spirit of self-righteousness* to muffle your testimony.

In Luke 18:9 the Bible says that Jesus was telling this parable to some who were trusting in themselves. The New International Version of the Bible says they were "confident in their own righteousness." Our enemy, Satan, knows if he can get us to start believing we are the good people and other people are the bad people, we are the right people and other people are the wrong people, then the *spirit of self-righteousness* will render us ineffective in our witness for God. The truth is, in the vernacular of the young people, *we are not all of that.* Some of the same things we say about other people; we do ourselves, or have done ourselves. The only reason we are in church, or why we are doing better in some areas in our lives is not because we are so great, but because God is so good. God had mercy on us one day and Jesus came into our lives. But when the *spirit of self-righteousness* gets on us, guess what happens? Nobody gets to hear that message, nobody gets to hear our testimony because we are too busy worrying about how much better we are than someone else and how someone else does not measure up to our standards.

Somebody Ought to Testify

Who do you think you are that someone has to

measure up to your standards? Who do you think you are that someone else has to conform to the way you think things ought to be? The *spirit of self-righteousness* eventually leads to us forgetting all about God's standards and we start trying to impose our standards as though they were God's standards. We fail when we start to care less about whether or not people are walking in obedience to God than we do about how loud the music is in church. Do you really believe that God is worried about how loud the music is? Do you really believe God is worried about how short that sister's skirt is, or whether or not she is in church? Do you really believe that God is worried about how baggy that young brother's pants are, or whether or not that young man is in the house of the Lord instead of out on some street corner? When I was a teenager I used to wear my pants hanging off my behind too! Yes, I admit it! I, the pastor wore my pants off my behind when I was a teenager. But I grew up, and I grew out of it. The Bible says, "when I was a child I used to speak as a child, think as a child, reason as a child; but when I became a man I did away with childish things." (1 Corinthians 13:11) When I went to church, I had people who didn't specialize in telling me how bad I was. They specialized in telling me how good God is.

There ought to be some people in the house of the Lord who are not ashamed or afraid to say *'I am a testimony today. I smoked some reefer along the way, but I'm a testimony. I snorted some cocaine or smoked some crack along the way, but I'm a testimony. I had some one night stands with some people I didn't know, but I'm a testimony. I was a teenage mother but I'm a testimony. I spent some time in jail but I'm a testimony. I wasn't always sure about my sexuality, but*

I'm a testimony. I was abused as a child, but I'm a testimony. I didn't grow up in a church going family, but I'm a testimony. I told some lies, and gotten over on some people calling myself slick, but I'm a testimony.' Stop playing like you have been a saint all of your life. There are enough people around who knew you when you weren't as holy as you are today. When they see you, they shout because you are a testimony of what God can do. Somebody needs to hear that testimony.

Do you know the problem with the Pharisee in this parable of Jesus? He had a wonderful testimony. If he was living and doing all of those things he talked about in his prayer, then God had surely been good to him. God had blessed him and no doubt brought him from a mighty long way. But he got to the church and began to pray as though he had done it all himself. He began to pray as though those things made him a better person than the tax collector. His testimony should have helped bring the tax collector closer to God, not push him further away. Who is your testimony helping to bring to the Lord? Take back your life by reclaiming your testimony.

Don't Turn God's People Away!

Not only must we recognize that the spirit of self-righteousness muffles our testimony, but also it turns God's people away from God. What could Satan, enjoy more than to see God's people turn God's people away from God? This group to which Christ was speaking, in this parable had not only been trusting in their own righteousness, but they looked down on everybody else. *'But Pastor, I thought those of us who know Christ in the pardon of our sins are God's people.*

It sounds to me like you are saying even those who don't know Christ and who may be living lives in which God is not pleased are God's people too.' Psalm 24:1 says, "the earth is the Lords, and the fullness thereof, the world and all those who live in it." Jesus said in John 10:16, "other sheep have I and they are not of this fold, and them must I also bring." In other words, even those who are not saved yet, still belong to God.

You may not fully understand it all but you belong to God. You may not have grown up real *churchy*, but you still belong to God. You may not have done everything right in your life, but you still belong to God. Perhaps you have messed up and made some mistakes along the way, but you are still one of God's people. You may not even know it yet, but you are one of God's people.

I wish I knew some *other sheep* that could make some noise. "Baaah, I was out in the streets." "Baaah, I was out in the world." "Baaah, I was doing things I had no business doing, but praise be to God, Jesus came and got me one day."

The Bible says when the tax collector came to the temple and saw the Pharisee he stood at a distance. He knew his mere presence there offended the Pharisee. He knew he really was not welcome there. Just in case, he thought he might be welcomed, the Pharisee took care of all of that in his prayer, "Lord thank goodness, I am not like him."

It never ceases to amaze me how people in church can make people feel as though they had better not get too close. Don't get too close because we don't dress like that in our church. Don't get too close because we don't praise like that in our church. Don't get too close, because we don't sing that kind of music in our church. Don't get too close because we don't make that much noise in our church. Don't get too close, because we don't like to stay too long in our church. The *spirit of self-righteousness* is responsible for more empty churches across this country than anything else.

The church is where people are saved and hear the life changing, transforming Word of God. It is where people get their faith restored in spite of their circumstances. It is where people get power to overcome whatever the enemy may be trying to do in their lives. The church is where people come to get *"strength for today and bright hope for tomorrow."* What could possibly be more appealing to Satan, than to unleash self-righteousness in the church? I told you earlier to unleash your faith. Our self -righteousness needs to be put on a tight leash and kept in the yard. In fact why don't we just make the enemy mad and take our self-righteousness to the vet and have it put down. The enemy wants those who are hurting and in need of a breakthrough, those who are struggling through addictions, and illicit sexual behaviors, marital unrest, parental frustration and challenging health crises, to remain at a distance?

The saddest commentary of the prayer of the Pharisee is that the *spirit of self -righteousness* had such a powerful hold on him. Even after coming to church and acknowledging God, he left without getting what he needed most. He did not need a pat on the shoulder for the life he was living. What he needed most was not to be congratulated for being faithful and obedient to

God. There is no point in us thinking that we are doing God a favor by anything we do for God. God has been so good to us we can never repay the Lord for all of His goodness. What he needed most was to know he needed God. He needed to know God accepted and loved him even before he did all of those things. Romans 5:8 says, "while we were yet sinners, Christ died for us." It does not matter how good or how righteous we believe we are we still need God. It does not matter how much education we have or don't have, we still need God. It doesn't matter how many mistakes we have made along the way, we all need God. We need God, like the grass needs water. We need God, like the moon needs the sun. We need God like fish need the ocean. We need God, and the *spirit of self-righteousness* blinds us to the fact that no matter who we are we all need God. We overcome the *spirit of self-righteousness* when we recognize our sinful nature and need for Christ despite our good works. We also overcome the *spirit of self-righteousness* when we share our testimony of where God has brought us from, rather than acting like we did it by ourselves. By accepting the free gift of God in Christ Jesus, we eliminate the need to try to earn our salvation, because we have a Savior who has paid it all. Take back your life by overcoming the *spirit of self-righteousness.*

Prayer: Father Your Word teaches me my righteousness is a filthy rag to You. Remind me in those moments when I think more highly of myself than I should that it is not about me. Help me to live not being overly impressed with how good I am but always praising You for how awesome You are. I have a testimony of what You have done for me. Give me less of me and more of You. If I have turned someone away with my self-righteousness, please, forgive me. In Jesus Name. Amen!

Chapter Six

The Spirit of Ingratitude!

[I]n everything give thanks; for this is God's will for you in Christ Jesus. 1 Thessalonians 5:18 (NASB)

One of my favorite New Testament writers is the apostle Paul. He started out being very skeptical about Jesus. He did not accept everything the early believers said right away. He was not one of these perfect people who had been saved all of his life. He made some mistakes, and some bad choices. He spent some time with bad company which influenced him to do hurtful things to other people. There were some skeletons in his closet.

Despite his imperfections, Jesus still saw enough in him to use him to become the architect of New Testament theology. So I really admire Paul. His life story encourages those of us who are harder on ourselves than anyone else could ever be. Paul reminds us that when Jesus is in the equation of our life, even the worst of us can make a turn around, and a difference. It is because I admire Paul so much that it is difficult to say Paul appears to be mistaken in this particular case.

You Gotta Be Kidding Me!

I agree with most of what Paul has to say in the New Testament. I am encouraged by him when he says "now unto Him that is able to do exceeding abundantly beyond all that we ask or think, according to the power that works within us." (Ephesians 3:20) I celebrate with him when he declares that "my God shall supply all of your needs according to His riches in glory."

(Philippians 4:19) I am in agreement with him when he says that "God has not given us a spirit of fear, but of power and love and of a sound mind." (2 Timothy 1:7) I am convicted by him when he tells us that "all have sinned and fall short of the glory of God." (Roman 3:23)

However, in 1 Thessalonians I believe Paul must be mistaken. In the book of 1 Thessalonians Paul is writing to the church at Thessalonica. He is concluding his letter to them and he tells them "in everything give thanks for this is the will of God in Christ Jesus for you." (I Thessalonians 5:18) Perhaps it would help you to understand why I think Paul must have spoken incorrectly in this letter by telling you that Paul knew that the people in Thessalonica didn't have a whole lot to be thankful for.

Perhaps you know what it is to feel like you don't have much to be grateful for. Perhaps you would really like to say, *'Pastor, if you only knew what is going on in my life, and what I had to go through. My parents didn't treat me right. They really didn't love me. That is how I ended up all messed up like this, and now I have kids, and they are all messed up too. I am worried about them, and my life is just a total mess. Sometimes I don't even feel like getting out of the bed in the morning.'*

Thessalonica was the capital city of Macedonia. In Acts chapter 17 when Paul came to preach the good news that Christ had died for our salvation and was raised from the dead, he had started a church there. Not soon after he started that ministry, the *spirit of jealousy* showed up among people in Thessalonica. Some people said Paul was causing trouble and stirring up the people and they had to sneak Paul out of town. It got violent and the people who followed Jesus at the church in Thessalonica were under constant attack.

In addition, the Bible says in 2 Corinthians 8 they didn't have much money. You may be aware that nothing puts people in a bad mood like not having any money. Few things make a person depressed, upset, irritable, quiet, non-responsive, and down, like not having any money. When there is no money in the house, relations are strained between family members, tempers flare, and tensions are high. Some years ago there was a popular saying, *"romance without finance is nuisance."* Many marriages end in divorce because of money.

Maybe I shouldn't say they didn't have any money because they did have some money, but what is clear is they didn't have enough money. And that is even more stressful than having no money. Not having enough money gets us mad and aggravated. At least if I am completely broke, I am just broke. To have a little money but not enough money to do anything is really frustrating. I am talking about those times when there are 8 days between you and pay day and you have $12.00 to last those whole 8 days. They had some money but it was not enough to do the things they needed to do. The people at Thessalonica were being persecuted for what they believed, and they didn't have any real money.

Paul writes them this letter and says to these people, who are being dragged out of their houses and who don't have much money, "in everything give thanks." But I just know Paul could not be telling *these* people to give thanks. Certainly he could not be telling them to give thanks for being persecuted, and thanks for being broke. In fact I am so certain it must be a mistake I looked up the Greek word he uses in this verse to make sure it was not translated incorrectly by some later writer. It says Paul used the Greek word pas, which means everything, or all; it means nothing is left out but everything is included.

Ingratitude is a Weapon of Satan!

Paul knew what he was asking the people of Thessalonica to do sounded crazy. It still sounds crazy today. He also knew if he did not encourage their hearts to have a grateful spirit; the enemy would have the opportunity to inflict them with a *spirit of ingratitude*. Our parents and grandparents used to teach that lesson well. They would tell us to "count our many blessings, and name them one by one. Count our many blessings and look what God has done."

A *spirit of ingratitude* is more than just not saying thank you to God or to someone for a kind deed that they have done. A *spirit of ingratitude* is one of the weapons that our enemy, Satan, uses against us so we miss what God wants to do in our lives. I want to break the back of that ugly *spirit of ingratitude* in your life today. I bind ingratitude in your life in the Name of Jesus! By the help of Almighty God you may have conquered fear, doubt, self-destruction, jealousy, and self-righteousness, but in order to take back your life you must defeat the *spirit of ingratitude*. Satan has looked into your future and knows what God has in store for your life. He has determined that he will use any means at his disposal to prevent you from getting to where God is taking you. This is not because he cares about what God wants to give you, but because he wants to render you ineffective in witnessing for God. If the enemy can cause us to develop a spirit of ingratitude, then we won't feel like we have a testimony. If you think about the story of Job in the Bible you will recognize that the devil's strategy was to make Job so miserable that he would become ungrateful to God for all of his blessings. Satan tells God, "But now stretch out Your hand and touch all that he has, and he will surely curse You to your face." (Job1:12)

The devil wants to stop you. He knows that by stopping you he can stop a hundred other people who might be blessed by your testimony. If he has tried the *spirit of fear*, but you were not afraid; and tried the *spirit of doubt*, but you were sure that God was with you, he will keep trying. If he has tried the *spirit of jealousy*, but you got over it, and tried the spirit of *self-destruction*, but you were wise to his game, he will not give up. After he had tried to tempt Jesus he only left Him alone until "an opportune time." (Luke 4:13) He will try the *spirit of self-righteousness*. If you came to church and heard the pastor preach on it and you recovered, the devil will try something else. When the devil sees you have made it past all of those other spirits he uses to steal life from us, he will know that you are extremely grateful to God. He will say they know it was nothing but the hand of God that brought them through. But just in case, let me see if I can use this *spirit of ingratitude* to drive a wedge between them and God.

How Ingratitude Works

The *spirit of ingratitude* is much more powerful than we even believe. We basically think that ingratitude is about a person not having good home training. We write it off as someone not having parents who taught them to send thank you notes, or not having sense enough to recognize when God or some other person has been good to them. It is much more than that, because whenever you see a person suffering under a *spirit of ingratitude*, they are under the demonic influence of one of Satan's spirits.

We know what it feels like to be the recipients of ingratitude, it hurts. I am talking to some parents who are destroyed because they are thinking after all I have done for this child. Do they have any idea how many sacrifices I have made to try to give them a better life than I had? How can they be so ungrateful? I am talking to some wives and some husbands who are a ticking time bomb waiting to explode. You are thinking after all I have done for this person, how dare they have the nerve to act as though it is nothing to them?

I am talking to a person who has given years to a job, a company, a career, only to have some people come along who do not value, appreciate, or respect you. They have no idea what those years took from you that no amount of paycheck can compensate. Now you are wondering how they could dispense of you, as though your life meant nothing. The *spirit of ingratitude* is more than bad manners, poor parenting, or personal selfishness. It is an indication that our enemy, Satan, has found a way to attack, hinder, or prevent us from all that God wants to do in our lives.

Paul Wasn't Wrong After All

Here comes mister happy go lucky Paul, who nothing seems to bother. Paul was in and out of prison in the cause of Christ Paul, and he was alright. His message is in everything give thanks. Would you mind if I questioned Paul a little bit on his advice? I am sorry, Paul, but it just seems like there ought to be some exemptions to this giving thanks in everything. If I could have a conversation with Paul I would tell him what I think. If people don't treat me right, Paul, I ought to get an exemption! Paul might say *"Give thanks!"* What if people tell lies about me is that exempt? *"Give thanks!"* What if someone gossips on me and it is not even true? I know that's exempt! *"Give thanks!"* What about if people gossip on me and it is true? *"Give thanks!"* Well, what if somebody does something hurtful to a member of my family, Paul; I know I can have an exemption for that? *"In everything give thanks!"* Well, Paul, I have a problem with that. If somebody does something to somebody in my family, what do I look like giving thanks? They had better look out!

But notice what Paul says, he does not say give thanks for everything, even though he does tell us in Romans "that all things work together for good for those who love the Lord for those who are the called according to His purpose." (Romans 8:28) He does not say give thanks for everything. He says give thanks in everything. When we give thanks in everything it simply means there is not a thing that we can be in that God won't be in with us. God, I am in a *whole hot mess*, but I can give thanks because I know You are right there with me. Jesus, I am in a tight spot. But You told me You would never leave me nor forsake me. I can give thanks, not for the tight spot, but in the tight spot, because no matter how tight it gets I know I am not by myself. If you and I are going to take authority over the *spirit of ingratitude* that prevents us from becoming who God is calling us to be then, as crazy as it sounds we have got to learn how to give God thanks in everything. This was not just talk for Paul. He actually had to practice what he preached. He shares just a little of what he experienced when he talks about suffering with a thorn in his flesh. Finally, after seeking the Lord three times for relief and getting none, Paul concludes, "Therefore I take pleasure in my infirmities in reproaches, in needs, in persecutions, in distresses, for Christ's sake. For when I am weak, then I am strong." (1Corinthians 12:12)

A Turtle on a Tree Stump

The *spirit of ingratitude* is often rooted in a sense of personal accomplishment. If I feel like my success was achieved by my own effort then I don't have any reason to be thankful. If I feel as though I am the reason for my success, my accomplishments, and my blessings, then I will have very little reason to be thankful to God or to anybody else. Many of us would never come out and say we think we did it all alone because we know it sounds ugly. However, our actions towards God and others often display our true feelings. We really do think we are *self-made.* You sound like a fool talking about, I'm a *self-made man,* or I'm a *self-made woman.* You are a *self-made fool* if you think that way. All we remember is the late nights, early mornings, second jobs, or the ramen noodles that we ate along the way. We forget God and the people God used to bless us, and help us get to where we could have never gotten by ourselves. Incidentally, the *spirit of ingratitude* is always easier to recognize in others than it is in ourselves.

Many people misunderstand tithing as an act of

thanks to God. They think I am the one that went to school. I am the one that worked those hours. I am the one that made those sacrifices. And now you are telling me I am supposed to give 10% of my money? Well, let me answer that question with a question, who made it possible for you to go to school? Who enabled you to have a place to work? And who gave you the strength to hold on while you were making those sacrifices? It was the Lord, in case you didn't know. If we always think that it was what we did, then we will always be candidates for our enemy, Satan, to use the *spirit of ingratitude* in our lives. Take back your life by refusing to believe the lie that you have made it all by yourself.

One of my earliest mentors in ministry and in life was a great man of God the renowned Samuel Dewitt Proctor. Dr. Proctor used to ask a question which illustrates our condition beautifully. He would ask, "Have you ever seen a turtle on top of a tree stump?" Of course the answer would come back, "No." He would respond, "If you ever do, the one thing you know is the turtle did not get there by himself. He had some help along the way." You did not get to where you are by yourself. Don't let the enemy cause you to think you climbed your tree stumps without any help.

In my life and times, I have been in some bars. In a bar, there is a protocol. The bartender makes you a drink; you give them a dollar tip when you pay for your drink. One drink is given a one dollar tip. Two drinks are given a two dollar tip, and so on. Some people would never consider not giving the bartender that one dollar tip for a drink. Now notice that you paid for the drink, in fact you probably paid too much for it. But you bought it, and then you gave a dollar tip. How should that make us feel about tithing when we consider the salvation God has given us was paid for by Jesus? We did not earn salvation. We did not buy deliverance. We did not deserve forgiveness, and we are not worthy of it, but Jesus paid it. If we are going to take authority over the *spirit of ingratitude* in our lives, we have got to stop thinking whatever we have or don't have, achieved or not achieved, accomplished or not accomplished, has been done on our own.

Ingratitude Accentuates the Negative!

We also need to understand that our enemy, Satan, will use the *spirit of ingratitude* by always pointing out what is missing in our lives. Satan wants to shift our focus away from what God has already done for us. If your enemy, the devil, can keep you from looking at your life and saying my good days may not always out number my bad days, but they always outweigh my bad days, then the enemy can allow a *spirit of ingratitude* to creep into your spirit. If the devil can keep us focused on what we don't have, how much money we need for this item, or how much money we need for that bill, then a *spirit of ingratitude* can creep in. If our minds are made to concentrate on how somebody else was able to get a new car and we still have an old one, or all of the reasons why we believe we cannot afford to put God first in our finances then the *spirit of ingratitude* can get a foothold in our spirit.

I have met many amazing people in my life. One of the most amazing is a member of our congregation. He is a double amputee. As a pastor I have seen what losing just one leg has done to people, let alone two. He has an awesome spirit. He never talks about how horrible it is to be a double amputee but he does talk about loving God, loving his church, and helping to guide and support the young people. He loves to talk about how good God has been to him. For years I visited him at home because he did not have a way to get to church. Finally he was able to get a van that could accommodate his needs. A lot of people would have gotten that van and been everywhere but church on Sunday morning. Since he got that van he has barely missed a Sunday of church. He is more faithful in his church attendance than a whole lot of people who have two legs but are suffering from a *spirit of ingratitude*.

Take back your life by refusing to focus on the areas of lack in your life. These areas of lack may be monetary, family, health, loneliness, opportunity, fulfillment, or companionship. We all have some areas in which we would love to see the Lord move in our life but as long as we only focus on those wants, we will always be candidates for the *spirit of ingratitude* to steal life from us.

Ingratitude Can Short Circuit Your Favor!

We need to understand why Paul says in everything give thanks. None of us receives anything because we are so wonderful. None of us receives anything because we are so great, awesome, or got it all together. The only way any of us accomplishes anything in life is God gives us favor with other people. When other people have favor on us, we get the house our credit could not afford. When other people have favor on us we are made aware of opportunities we would never have known about. When other people give us favor we get customers for our business just because of someone else's word. When other people have favor on us, we get access in areas we never even knew existed. Favor is when God blesses us through one another. When God gives you favor with someone you can you go from being unemployed to having a job.

Satan knows that he cannot stop God from giving you favor with other people. So what does the enemy do? The enemy gives us an ungrateful spirit, a *spirit of ingratitude*, because a *spirit of ingratitude* dries up the favor. Think about it. Nobody wants to help an ungrateful person. People don't want to do things for an ungrateful person. A person who has a *spirit of ingratitude* becomes their own enemy by working for their worst enemy, Satan. Satan can't stop God from blessing you and giving you favor with people. But you and I can make other people not want to be bothered with us by our own ungrateful spirit towards them. The *spirit of ingratitude* grows like black mold in the dark corners of our spirit. Satan is trying to use the *spirit of ingratitude* in us to suffocate the favor that God has given us with other people.

Bishop TD Jakes of Dallas, Texas made a valuable contribution to my understanding on favor when he told us that "favor is not fair." Pastor R.A. Vernon of the Word Church in Cleveland, Ohio, enhanced my understanding when he told us that "favor also is not free." I want to make my own contribution to your understanding of favor by simply stating that, in addition to not being fair, and not being free; favor is not necessarily forever. If the *spirit of ingratitude* becomes resident in our lives, it dries up the favor. Keep the favor of God and man upon you and take back your life, by having an attitude of gratitude.

Prayer: Lord open my eyes and my heart to see the many blessings You have showered upon me. I know Lord that I did not get here by myself. You have kept, preserved, protected, and provided for me all the days of my life. I rebuke the thought of the devil that makes me foolishly think I am self-made. I am nothing without You and I need Your favor. Make my life and not just my words an expression of my gratitude for all that You are to me. In Jesus Name. Amen!

Chapter Seven

The Holy Spirit

"But you Shall receive power when the Holy Spirit has come upon you; and you shall be witnesses to Me in Jerusalem, and in all Judea and Samaria, and to the end of the earth." Acts 1:8 (NKJV)

Now that You Know

Satan's purpose is to disconnect us from our destiny in God. He will use every fair or unfair method at his disposal to accomplish this purpose through our own ignorance to what is going on in our lives. If we do not recognize what the enemy is doing, we miss the point that we are in spiritual warfare when he attacks. "For our struggle is not against flesh and blood, but against the rulers, against the powers, against the world forces of this darkness, against the spiritual forces of wickedness in the heavenly places." (Ephesians 6:12) Stop thinking that every incident of adversity in your life is about someone disliking you. It is, but that someone is the devil. Just as you don't bring a knife to a gun fight, you don't bring fleshly weapons to a spiritual war.

We surrender life by attributing the devil's attacks to other things. The only way to have power over the attacks of the devil is to recognize what spirit he is using to steal life from you. Hosea 4:6 says, "My people are destroyed for the lack of knowledge." What we don't know can hurt us.

Once you recognize how the devil operates, you can take back your life from him. We know that the *spirit of ingratitude* dries up the favor that God gives us with other people. So we must be careful not to allow that spirit into our lives. We know that the *spirit of jealousy* never shows up dressed as what it really is, so we must look beneath the surface of actions and words to see if the *spirit of jealousy* is at work. We know that the *spirit of fear* shows up when we are about to accomplish something great in God. This book is about taking back your life, by taking authority over the spirits of the enemy.

Intruder Alert!

Our Father has provided us with an intruder alert system for when those spirits enter the building of our lives, He is called Holy Spirit. Most of us are familiar with alarm systems. We have them on our cars and in our homes. They serve an important purpose. They alert us that someone who may not belong there has entered the premises. Someone with bad intentions is about to steal something from us. The Holy Spirit is our spiritual intruder alert from God. Going through life without the Holy Spirit is inviting the devil to steal life from you. Jesus promised Him to us and told His disciples that the Holy Spirit would live with us, and be in us. (John 14:17) Jesus also said that the Holy Spirit would guide us into all truth. (John 16:13)

In the book of Acts, we see the Holy Spirit at work in the formation of the church and in the formation of the men and women who shaped the church. Acts 2:4 tells us that the disciples were filled with the Holy Spirit on the day of Pentecost. Pentecost was a Jewish feast which means, fiftieth day. It celebrated the giving of the law to Moses at Mt. Sinai. Acts 2:41 tells us that on the day of Pentecost after being filled with the Holy Spirit Peter delivered a sermon in which 3000 souls were added to the kingdom. The fifth Chapter of Acts tells the unfortunate story of a husband and wife, Ananias, and Sapphira, who lied to the Holy Spirit and met with dire consequences. Throughout the book of Acts there are examples of the Holy Spirit at work.

A Weak Resume

Jesus' disciples were not impressive. To be completely honest about it, Jesus didn't leave the Holy Spirit with much to work with. The disciples had a weak resume. No one would think they were capable of accomplishing anything great. Throughout Matthew, Mark, Luke, and John, the picture of the disciples is of weak and indecisive men. They are portrayed as narrow minded, greedy, selfishly ambitious, fearful, and lacking faith and power. There are several times when Jesus describes them as "ye of little faith." One time after they had been ineffective with casting out a demon from a boy, Jesus asks "how long must I stay with these disciples of mine." (Luke 9:41)

Out on the water the disciples were all fearful. (Matthew 8:25) After His resurrection Thomas was doubtful. (John 20:25) Judas became so jealous of Jesus that he betrayed Him and later killed himself in the ultimate act of self-destruction. (John 12:4, Matthew 27:5) James and John were so self-righteous they thought they should sit one on His left hand and the other on His right. (Mark 10:37) All of them abandoned Him when He needed them the most. During Jesus' arrest and trial, Peter, Jesus' closest disciple, only followed Jesus at a distance. (Matthew 26:58) After all Jesus had done for them, they were ungrateful. They were so pitiful they went back to fishing. That's what they were doing before Jesus came into their lives. (John 21:3)

From Matthew through John, the disciples of Jesus were not impressive. Truthfully, those women whom Jesus had around him were much stronger, had more faith, and were more committed than any of the disciples Jesus chose. (Luke 8:1-3) Despite their imperfections the first disciples of Jesus were in many ways similar to modern day followers of Christ. The disciples were like us. If we look closely, we can see ourselves in them. That is why we don't really want to be too hard on the disciples of Jesus, because a close examination reveals that we have much in common.

Drop Your Stone and Walk Away

Jesus' disciples were raggedy sometimes, but aren't we all? If someone were to take the time to write down in the pages of a book, all of the dysfunction, fear, jealousy, doubt, self-destructive, and self-righteous behavior we do on a daily basis, some reader would ask, "what kind of people are these?" If walls could talk and tell some of the things we have done, and shoes could talk and tell some of the places we have been, we would all have to drop our stones and walk away. The Bible says that when Jesus caught men about to stone a woman who had been caught in adultery, He told them the one without sin should cast the first stone. They were so convicted by His words that one by one they walked away. (John 8:9) I am not going to be the first to throw a stone at Jesus' disciples. I understand what it is to not have it all together just yet.

What stands out the most about Jesus disciples

is not how extraordinary they were but how ordinary. Jesus' disciples were very similar to us. Jesus didn't go out and choose a bunch of Ivy League graduates, rocket scientists, or all-stars to be His disciples. He went and got regular, ordinary men with all of the human frailties and weaknesses that are so common to us all. Levi was a tax collector, a hated profession. (Luke 5:27) Simon, Andrew, James and John were fisherman. (Mark 1:16-20)

But when we get to the Book of Acts, Jesus takes those ordinary and imperfect disciples, and does extraordinary things through them. So much so, that at one point they are described in the Bible as those who "turned the world upside down." (Acts 17:6) Knowing their weaknesses, faults, and frailties, how could these same men whom we encounter in the pages of the gospel writers, have such an impact on the world?

Something Got Hold of Me

Something happened to them along the way. Something got hold of them in between the resurrection of Jesus, and the founding of the church. Something came alive in them that changed everything about them and gave them a new outlook, attitude, and power. Something happened that enabled them to take back their lives. Actually, someone got hold of the disciples, called the Holy Spirit.

In Acts chapter 1 the disciples were all together in Jerusalem. And Jesus appeared to them one final time and made them one final promise, "but you shall receive power after that the Holy Spirit has come upon you, and you shall be witnesses to Me in Jerusalem, and in all Judea, and Samaria, and to the end of the earth."

(Acts 1:8) The record of the Book of Acts is when the Holy Spirit came upon them, they spoke with other tongues and the multitude gathered there for the festival was shocked because they each heard them in their own language. (Acts 2:6) They had power like they never knew before. Multitudes of people came to know Jesus in the pardoning of their sins, people were healed, and the church grew daily. (Acts 2:47) But that was only the beginning.

Watch Out World!

The Holy Spirit directed the disciples in establishing the Christian church. The Holy Spirit was even active in selecting leaders for the church who had not been part of Jesus' original twelve disciples. (Acts 13:2) One of those leaders was the Apostle Paul who had been a persecutor of the early church. Paul speaks of being compelled by the Holy Spirit to go to Jerusalem in spite of the danger associated with the trip. Paul says that the Holy Spirit "testifies in every city, telling me that chains and tribulations await me." (Acts 20:24-25) The Holy Spirit gave them boldness in spite of their detractors. (Acts 4:31) The Spirit went ahead of them and opened doors, prepared the way, and made friends for them in places they did not know, among people they did not know. The Holy Spirit protected them from dangers seen and unseen, by warning them where to go and where not to go. (Acts 11:12, 16:6)

The six previous spirits mentioned in this book are the weapons of Satan. They steal life from us when we are unaware of their presence and their methods. The Holy Spirit is the gift Jesus left us to lead us into all truth, so we will not be deceived by the attacks of the devil. (John: 16:7-15)

If the Holy Spirit could take disciples with little faith and use them to turn the world upside down, then just imagine what the Holy Spirit can do in you. We may be more like those disciples than we care to admit. But even if we are, if the Holy Spirit could use them to turn the world upside down, just imagine what He will do in this world through us.

After the Crash

The disciples were beat up emotionally after the murder of Jesus. They were a wreck. We know they were a wreck, because Judas had betrayed Jesus, and Peter had denied even knowing Him. (Matthew 26:47-50, 69-75) After three years of study and labor with Christ, seeing Him murdered on a cross caused the disciples to emotionally crash. Experiencing a crash after a traumatic event is something we all encounter in life.

When I was a boy I loved the Six Million Dollar Man. I had the plaid shirt, the bell bottom pants, and the lunch box to prove it. His name was Steve Austin. He was an astronaut who went on a mission and crashed. The crash he experienced almost killed him. He should have died but the government took the opportunity to use what was left to create the world's first "bionic man."

When the doctors rebuilt Steve Austin, they made him better. They gave him a left eye with a zoom lens, which meant he could see much farther than any normal eye could see. That eye also had an infrared filter which allowed him to see in the dark and to detect heat. They gave Steve Austin a right arm that was as strong as a bulldozer. That strength meant he was much stronger than he had been before the crash. Then they gave Steve Austin legs that made him run about 60 miles per hour. He had crashed and he almost died, but he came out stronger, faster and with the ability to see more than he ever could before the crash.

Do you know what it is to crash? Do you know what it is to have everything fall apart, and to have the whole bottom fall out? A crash is when you lose your job, or your marriage goes haywire, or the doctor gives a diagnosis of cancer. Crashes are those moments in life when we feel like we are falling apart. It is when you are having an emotional breakdown, and the pressure of life is overwhelming, and your children are following their self -destructive friends rather than listening to you. Do you know what it is to crash?

The disciples had crashed. They believed that Jesus was going to be a conquering king, and He was crucified like a common criminal. There was a major disconnection between their idea of Jesus and what they had just experienced. God had revealed to Peter that Jesus was the Christ, the Son of the living God. (Matthew 16:16-17) Two other disciples James and John had been bold enough to request a seat on the right and left hand of Jesus. (Mark 10:37) Yet, there Jesus hung on an old rugged cross. The disciples had crashed. Even when they knew He had risen from the dead, they didn't really understand what that was all about, and what it meant for them as they moved forward. John records that in the midst of their emotional turmoil like many of us they sought the familiar and the comfortable, they went fishing. (John 21:3) They had crashed. Sometimes we all crash in life. And like Steve Austin, many of those crashes should have been our

Jesus knew they were in no shape to go out and change the world. That's why He told them to just go to Jerusalem and wait. Don't do anything just stay there and wait until the Holy Spirit comes upon you. (Luke 24:49) They didn't have the whole story. Jesus said the Holy Spirit would lead us into all truth. (John 16:13) The Holy Spirit remakes us. When the Holy Spirit comes alive inside of us, we become like that six million dollar man, we have new power.

I Don't See It That Way

Fear, doubt, self-destruction, jealousy, self-righteousness, and ingratitude steal life from us by causing us to see ourselves the way Satan wants us to. Take back your life by awakening to the power and availability of the Holy Spirit and telling the devil, I don't see it that way. Through the power of the Holy Spirit you can see some aspects of God at work in your life you could not see before. Without the Holy Spirit, I cannot see what the enemy was trying to do in my life. But when the power of the Holy Spirit is at work in my life, I can recognize what the enemy is trying to do. The Holy Spirit empowers us to see beyond our present reality. If you have ever watched a 3D movie then you know there are special glasses you wear for the movie. You can watch a 3D movie without the glasses and know the story, characters, setting and even how it ends. When you put 3D glasses on, you begin to see aspects of the same movie that you never saw before. If all I can see is where I am right now, then when I crash, my crash will kill me. The Holy Spirit enables us to see beyond what is right in front of us. Maybe you have crashed; emotionally, physically, financially, mentally or spiritually, but Jesus gave us the Holy Spirit as a means of being in constant communion with Him. With the Holy Spirit inside of you, you can see more for yourself in God. Take back your life through the power of the Holy Spirit.

One Crash from a Breakthrough

When they remade Steve Austin, they gave him an arm that could carry more. If you would have asked those disciples of Jesus at the end of John's gospel what was really going on, they would have said they had reached their limit. They had reached their breaking point. All of us have a breaking point. We may be able to put up with a lot, take a lot, look past, or ignore a lot, but there is not one of us who does not have a breaking point.

I have never hit a woman in my life. It is one of the things my mother instilled in me all my life. Men do not hit women. However, once while in high school while driving up a major street, I was dating a young lady and we were having a disagreement. She reached over, snatched my eye glasses off my face, and threw them out of the car window onto the street. I stopped the car because I actually need my glasses to drive. I pulled over. I got out of the car. I walked over to the passenger side of the car. I opened the door and I assisted her out of the vehicle. All of us have a breaking point.

The Holy Spirit will empower you to carry more than you ever thought you could carry and make you much stronger than you ever knew you could be. The Holy Spirit enables us to do more than we could ever do by ourselves.   You may be one crash away from receiving power like you have never known before. You may be one crash away from being able to say, *'the enemy thought he was going to break me, but God wanted to give me the Holy Spirit to bring me into closer relationship with Him.'* You may feel like you have reached your breaking point. Ask God right now to fill you with His Holy Spirit.

Plug Into His Power!

The Holy Spirit is not some abstract something out there in the somewhere as many people think. The Holy Spirit is the Spirit of God. From that perspective the Holy Spirit is always everywhere at all times. You have electricity running through your home. When you plug your appliance into one of the many electrical outlets in your home you receive power. The outlet is not the electricity. The outlet is the vehicle through which the electric current travels. It provides light, heat, and energy. The Holy Spirit is available to all believers. It is a tragedy that more followers of Christ don't plug into the power of God's Holy Spirit by asking Him to come into our lives. Going through life unplugged is no way for a Christian to live.   Pray for the Holy Spirit. Ask God to give you the Holy Spirit. Call upon the Lord and ask Him to fill you with the Holy Spirit. The Bible says God is a "rewarder of those who diligently seek Him." (Hebrews 11:6)   When the disciples of Jesus received the Holy Spirit, they were not engaged in some elaborate ceremony. The Bible says they were all together, and on one accord. (Acts 2:6) They went where Jesus had told them to go, and they stayed there and prayed and waited. Ask God for the Holy Spirit.

When the apostle Paul was in Ephesus he

encountered Christians who told him they had not even
heard whether there was a Holy Spirit. (Acts 19:2) Paul
baptized them in the Name of Jesus, laid hands on them
and they received the Holy Spirit and began to
prophesy and speak with tongues. (Acts 19:4-6)
Sometimes we live with less power than is available to
us. Like those Ephesians, we do not know what to ask
for. Ask God for the Holy Spirit. In Acts chapter 8,
Peter and John go down to Samaria to meet some new
believers in that region. The Bible says these new
believers had not yet received the Holy Spirit. Peter and
John prayed for them, laid hands on them, and they
received the Holy Spirit. (Acts 8:14-17) Ask God in
prayer to receive the Holy Spirit.

One of the most difficult truths for people to
accept is the fact that God will give His Spirit to us if
we ask. I was at my family reunion talking with some
cousins. One of my cousins was sharing how she
overcame smoking cigarettes. She had smoked
cigarettes for years and could not stop. One day she
asked God to remove it from her and she was delivered
from smoking cigarettes that very day. Many years
have passed, and now my cousin cannot even stand the
smell of cigarette smoke. What was amazing to me was
not her story. I know what God can do. What amazed
me were the people around the table. They asked her
repeatedly what she had to do to stop. It was as though
asking God to remove the desire to smoke was too
simple a solution to work. We are often guilty of
similar thinking when it comes to receiving God's Holy
Spirit. Something in us wants to make it more
complicated than asking God to give us His Holy Spirit.
Deliverance from whatever has you bound, clear
guidance for the decisions that perplex you, and healing

from the diseases that hurt you, are available to you when you ask our Father with a heart of faith.

Take It Back!

They gave the six million dollar man a new eye, to see beyond his present reality. They gave him a new arm, to enable him to carry more and make him stronger. They gave him new legs, to run faster and go further. He received legs that would not get tired. I don't care who you are, if you run too much you will get tired. Your legs will cramp up and say, "Hey, enough is enough." But they gave him legs that would not get tired. Look at what Jesus tells His disciples. "But you shall receive power after that the Holy Spirit has come upon you. And you shall be witnesses to me in Jerusalem, and in All Judea and in Samaria, and to the end of the earth." (Acts 1:8)

Jesus disciples could not even stay awake when He was in the garden praying. Jesus said to them, 'can't you guys even stay awake to keep watch while I go and pray.' (Matthew 26:40) Jesus tells them, when the Holy Spirit comes upon you, you will be My witnesses here locally but also to the ends of the earth. We want the Holy Spirit because the Holy Spirit enables us to go further than we could have ever imagined ourselves going. Jesus took those disciples and through the work of the Holy Spirit, used them to carry the good news Jesus saves down through 2000 years. He used them to turn the world upside down. How did it happen? Jesus gave them the extraordinary power of the Holy Spirit. 2000 years later, the church they helped start is still here, still growing, still going, still transforming lives, still making a difference, and still turning the world upside down.

If the Holy Spirit could work through Jesus' disciples, just imagine what the Holy Spirit can work through you to do today. Jesus wants to use the Holy Spirit to make a testimony out of you. You may not have finished high school, but you are going to make sure your children graduate college. Jesus wants to make a testimony out of you. That boy's daddy may not be worth a plug nickel, but you are going to raise that boy to be a man who respects himself, respects women, and supports his family. Jesus wants to make a testimony out of you. The doctor said it was cancer. *'Go and get your house in order, and get your things together, because it may not be long.'* But here you are, still going strong, you outlived the doctor, you out lived the nurse, you outlived the cancer. Jesus wants to make a testimony out of you. The devil thought he was going to break you when that person you loved, and trusted, betrayed you. Jesus wants to make a testimony out of you. It was bad enough when you got sick, but then your child got sick, you thought you would break. Jesus wants to make a testimony out of you. You have a mortgage to pay, a car note, car insurance, student loans, credit card debt, children in school, and gas prices are through the roof. Here comes the pastor talking about the Bible says give the first 10% of your income to God in tithes. You wonder how will you ever do all of that, but Jesus through the work of the Holy Spirit, wants to make a testimony out of you.

I want the Holy Spirit, because I am nobody, but by the Holy Spirit working through me the world will know that Jesus is somebody. I don't have any power, but by the power of the Holy Spirit working through me the world will know that Jesus has all power. Do you want to receive the Holy Spirit? Do you want to come back from your crash with more power than you ever had? Are you ready to take back your life from the traps the enemy has for you? Are you ready to turn your pitfalls into pit stops? Then ask God for His Holy Spirit.

God rewards those who diligently seek Him. Jesus told His disciples to go to Jerusalem and wait for the Holy Spirit. He told them not to do anything else until they had received the Holy Spirit. Take back your life through the power of the Holy Spirit. Even with all of your faults, failings, and shortcomings, your life will become a testimony to the power of Jesus to exercise extraordinary power through ordinary people. Not only will you take back your life, you will take on a new life that is even better than before.

Prayer: Father God, in the Name of Jesus, give me your Holy Spirit. Holy Spirit come into my life. Lead me and direct me in all that I do. Convict me when I try to take over and do it my way. Take over my mind, will, and emotions. Lead me in the way You would have me to go. Grow me into the mature servant you have called me to be. Open me up to receive, experience, and be refreshed by You. Let me lose my life to You so that I may gain my life. In Jesus Name. Amen!

ABOUT THE AUTHOR

Martin D. Odom mdodom134@gmail.com is a third generation Pastor in the African Methodist Episcopal Church. He is a graduate of Princeton Theological Seminary, and contributing writer to many newspapers and magazines. Martin enjoys reading books, watching football, and seeing people grow in their faith. He and his wife Nicole have two beautiful daughters, Maya and Samantha whom he lovingly calls "bossy" and "busy".

www.ingramcontent.com/pod-product-compliance
Lightning Source LLC
Chambersburg PA
CBHW051840040426
42447CB00006B/618